LOOK AT OUR LIVES:
STUDENT TWINNING
WITH PALESTINE

نظرة على حياتنا:
توأمة طلبة الجامعات
مع فلسطين

Look at our Lives:
Student Twinning with Palestine

EDITED BY NANDITA DOWSON
AND ABDUL WAHAB SABBAH

نظرة على حياتنا:
توأمة طلبة الجامعات
مع فلسطين

المحتويات   Contents

إهداء

تخليدا لذكرى معتصم عدوان طالب في كلية الصحافة والإعلام في جامعة القدس استشهد في الأول من آب من العام ٢٠١١

لم نكن نتوقع أن تكون القضية الأولى التي سيعرضها طلاب فلسطين عن حياتهم للطلاب من بريطانيا هي قضية استشهاد طالب من جامعة القدس بعد أن أطلق الجنود الاسرائيليون النار عليه من مسافة قصيرة جداً. حدث ذلك خلال فترة التحضير للمشروع، عندما كنا نعمل مع طلاب جامعة القدس وبالتحديد حول التحديدات التي تواجه الطلاب الذين يعيشون تحت الاحتلال العسكري في فلسطين وطلاب بريطانيا.

ففي الأول من آب استشهد الطالب معتصم عدوان ٢٢ عام طالب في كلية الإعلام في جامعة القدس أبوديس بعد إطلاق جنود إسرائيليون النار عليه من مسافة ٢٠ متر بجانب منزله في مخيم قلنديا. عندما كان يحتفل مع المئات من المواطنين باليوم الأول من رمضان، اقتحم الجيش الاسرائيلي مخيم قلنديا للاجئين حيث قام الجنود بإطلاق الرصاص الحي بدون أي تحذير للمواطنين وبدون أي مقاومة.

الحقيقة أن معتصم هو ضحية أخرى من الشبان الفلسطينيين الذين استشهدوا على أيدي الجيش الاسرائيلي وكون العائلة تعرف أنه لا توجد عدالة لدى الاحتلال فإنهم لم يتقدموا بأي مطالبات قانونية أو أي دعاوي ضد القتلة، ولم يتلقوا أي دعم يذكر في الوقت الذي كانوا فيه بأمس الحاجة للدعم بعد فقدان ابنهم حيث لم يعقدوا أي آمال على عدالة جيش محتل. في اليوم الذي أستشهد فيه معتصم أستشهد أيضا شاب آخر فيما أصيب ثالث بطلقة نارية بالرأس، كان هدف الجيش الاسرائيلي هو اعتقال مطلوبين وقد قام الجيش باعتقال اثنين من أبناء المخيم ولم يكن لمعتصم والشهيد الثاني ولا حتى المصاب أي علاقة بالمعتقلين.

تتقدم جمعية صداقة كامدن ابوديس وكل من شارك في مشروعنا بالتعازي الحارة لعائلة معتصم ولأصدقائه ولزملاء دراسته، نحن حزينين جداً لخسارة معتصم ولمن استشهد وأصيب معه.

لقد تم إهداء هذا الكتاب لذكرى معتصم٧

viii

Dedication

In memory of Motassem Odwan, media studies student from Al Quds University: shot and killed by Israeli soldiers on August 1st 2011.

We did not expect that the first thing the Palestinian students would need to share with the British students was the killing of a student from the Al Quds University, shot by soldiers at point-blank range. But this happened during the preparation phase of this project, while we were working with students from the Al Quds University, putting into sharp focus the different risks faced by students living under military occupation in Palestine and students in Britain.

On 1st August 2011, the first day of Ramadan, Motassem Odwan, aged 22, a student of media studies at the Al Quds University in Abu Dis, was shot dead by Israeli soldiers from a distance of 20 metres near his home in Qalandia Refugee Camp. He was out with thousands of others near their houses, celebrating the evening on the first of Ramadan when the Israeli army invaded the refugee camp. The Israeli soldiers shot live ammunition with no warning in a context where there was no resistance.

The fact is that Motassem is sadly one of many young Palestinians shot and killed by the Israeli army. The family did not ask for an enquiry or any support for his loss, as they have no expectations from the army of occupation, which acts with impunity. At the time that Motassem was shot, another young man was also killed and a third seriously wounded with a bullet in his head. The army had decided to arrest two people and these three were nothing to do with this at all.

Camden Abu Dis Friendship Association and everyone involved in the project send their huge sympathy to the family of Motassem and to his friends and fellow students. We are deeply saddened at his loss and at the death and injury to the others who were with him.

This book is dedicated to the memory of Motassem.

تكريم
معتصم

من كلمة ألقاها طالب نيابة عن الطلاب الفلسطينيين خلال الزيارة الى لندن

مرت ثلاث أشهر ونصف منذ أن رحل عنا صديقنا العزيز معتصم عدوان، لقد كان طالب مبتهج وضحوك في كلية الإعلام في جامعة القدس حيث كان يدرس ليصبح صحفي في المستقبل، على اعتبار إيمانه الراسخ بأن الصحافة هي سلاح للحقيقة وهي فرصة للتواصل من أجل السلام، والتي يغشاها أي احتلال غاشم في أي مكان في العالم ويحاول إسكاته.

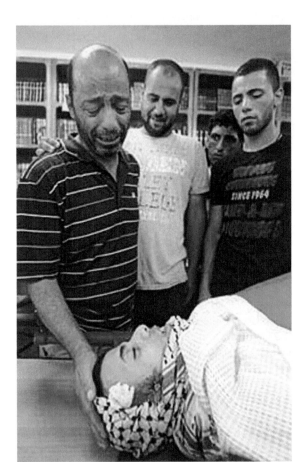

لقد كان في الأول من آب والذي صادف أول أيام رمضان عندما اقتحم جيش الدفاع الإسرائيلي مخيم قلنديا للاجئين كما اعتادوا أن يفعلوا بشكل مستمر بهدف اعتقال بعض الفتية الذي كانوا يلقون حجارة على دوريات عسكرية اسرائيلية محصنة. وعندما لم يجدوا هؤلاء الأطفال قرروا أن ينتقموا من أول شخص يعطيهم سبب وقد صادف أن كان هذا الشخص هو معتصم والذي كان يتحضر لامتحاناته ويأخذ فترة راحة قبل وجبة الإفطار في أول أيام رمضان.

عندما سمع صوت إطلاق النار خرج كما الجميع ليرى ما يحدث حيث كان إطلاق النار أمام بيته، عند وصوله الى خارج المنزل قام جاره بالصراخ عليه بان الجنود يصوبون بنادقهم عليه حيث استطاع ان يرى الليزر على جسده ولكن قبل ان يتحرك معتصم كان الجنود قد أطلقوا النار عليه برصاصتين بالرأس ورصاصة في القلب لتأكيد القتل، لتنتهي بهذا حياة وأحلام وآمال هذا الشاب، ولتبدأ مأساة عائلة كاملة وأصدقائه من الجامعة والنادي الرياضي الذي كان يتدرب فيه ليصبح بطل كمال أجسام.

متى يتوقف هذا القتل الممنهج والذي يهدد حياة شعبنا، سنبقى صامدين وسنذكر دائما من قضوا من شهداء وأبطال عبر السنوات الماضية، فلترقد بسلام يا معتصم عدوان.

X

Honouring Motassem

From a speech on behalf of the student visitors to London

Three months and a half passed since we lost a dear friend: Motassem. He was an ambitious, cheerful student of media sciences at Al-Quds University, who'd been studying to become a journalist, since he believed that journalism is a weapon of truth and communication to reach peace, which any oppressing occupation in the world fears and tries to silence.

It was the first of August, the first day of Ramadan, when the IDF (Israeli Defence Force) invaded Qalandia Refugee Camp as they do on a regular basis, to arrest some children who were throwing stones at their armoured vehicles. But since they couldn't find those, they decided to take revenge on the first person who gave them an excuse. It happened to be Motassem. He had been studying for his Media and International Relations exam before breaking his fast on the first of Ramadan.

Hearing gunshots outside his house, he ran outside to see what's going on. As he stood outside the door of his home, his neighbour started shouting; "They're pointing gun lasers at you! Watch out!" Before Motassem could react, the IDF sniper fired, shooting him in the head twice, and once in the heart, making sure he fell down motionless. To end a young man's dreams and hopes to be what he once wanted to be, and to start a traumatic tragedy for his family and friends at university and at the sports club he used to go to, where he worked hard to become a young body-builder.

Until such systematic murders and life threats to our people end, we will always stand our ground and we will remember the lives and the dreams of our heroes we've lost throughout the decades.

Rest in peace Motassem Odwan.

مشروع
نظرة
على
حياتنا

Look
at
our
lives

التوأمة مع فلسطين

من بريطانيا:

(كانت الرؤية أن يكون هناك علاقات توأمة بين كل موقع في فلسطين ومواقع بريطانية، بمعنى ان نوفر منبر لكل المواقع الفلسطينية من أجل إيصال صوتهم عندما يتعرضون لانتهاكات ضد حقوقهم الآدمية .)

مجتمعين سنحاول الوصول الى جميع المواقع في بريطانيا والتحدث الى آلاف الناس جامعين كل القصص والأحداث التي تعلمناها عن فلسطين، من أجل حثهم على التطلع الى ما يحدث في فلسطين والعمل من أجل نصرة قضايا حقوق الإنسان الفلسطيني.

من فلسطين:

(الصورة في مخيلتي عن ما تفعله التوأمة اننا وأصدقائنا من أبناء الشعب البريطاني نقف على حافتي وادي ننادي على بعضنا، وعندما أزور بريطانيا أستطيع أن أرى عدد الكبير من الناس في الوادي يتجاهلون ندائنا لكن مع مرور الوقت أرى الكثيرون يحاولون تسلق التلة للتواجد معنا والنظر الى ما يحدث لنا كفلسطينيين تحت الاحتلال ويقفون في نفس المكان مدافعين عن حقنا في الحياة .)

من أحد المشاركين في مشروع نظرة الى حياتنا:

نستطيع كلنا مشاهدة التأثير الكبير للتوأمة من خلال النشاطات التي توفرها .... ففي اليوم الذي أفتتح فيه معرض الصور، كان هناك

ورشة عمل بحضور العديد من ممثلي الطلبة في الجامعات اللندنية وما حول لندن، العديد من الأفكار طرحت للنقاش فيما يتعلق بالتوأمة وتطوير أدائها خاص فيما يتعلق بمجالس الطلبة وقد عملنا على وضع أجندنا مشتركة للعمل المستقبلي، خرج كل المتواجدين من الجامعات اللندنية من ورشة العمل بتوجه عام لضرورة العمل على الانخراط في عمل التوأمات ، تحديداً في الجامعات التي لا تحتفظ بعلاقة توأمة مع فلسطين.

بالاضافة الى ورشة العمل فقد زار الطلاب من فلسطين خلال رحلتهم العديد من الجامعات اللندنية وتحدثوا للطلاب عن حياتهم وضرورة عمل روابط توأمة وتواصل مع الطلبة البريطانيين في جامعاتهم.

Twinning with Palestine

From Britain:

"The vision is to build a twinning link between every place in Palestine and somewhere in Britain. This will mean that every place in Palestine will have somewhere to shout for them when there are violations of human rights.

"Between us we will spread across the ground in Britain with hundreds and thousands of people challenging the stories we were brought up with about the people of Palestine, looking clearly at what is happening there and working for human rights in Palestine."

From Palestine:

"I feel as if we and our British friends in the twinning movement are on hills shouting across a valley to each other. When I go to Britain I see how many people there are in the valley in between, ignoring the people on the hills. But every time I go I find that more of the people in the valley have climbed up on the hills and are looking at us, and starting to call out to us."

From a student in the 'Look at our Lives' project:

'We all saw what the benefits of twinning could be ... On the day of the photo exhibition, there was a twinning workshop attended by representatives of various universities in London and beyond, and many ideas and initiatives were discussed regarding the twinning of university unions. An agenda was set for the future, and the students from universities who did not yet have a twinning link went back with ideas on how to propose this, and the students who were at universities whose union indeed already had one gained new inspiration as to how to keep the twinning link alive and active. In addition to this meeting, the Palestinian students on their visits to universities during the week, emphasised the benefits of twinning and discussed this with the British students they met.'

مشروع نظرة على حياتنا

انطلق مشروع نظرة على حياتنا في بداية سنة ٢٠١١ حيث بدأنا العمل مع طلاب جامعة القدس في ابوديس وجامعات لندنية في كامدن من أجل إيجاد طرق لتعزيز التواصل وتقوية توأمات الطلبة، وقررنا بان يكون هناك تبادل مبني على مشروع للصور لنمكن الطلاب من الالتقاء والتعرف أكثر على حياة بعضهم وعلى ما هو متشابه ومختلف من تجاربهم كطلاب . اعتمد المشروع على أن يقوم الطلاب في الموقعين بالتقاط صور تمكنهم من مقارنة حياة الطلاب في الموقعين، ثم نقاش ما اكتشفوا وتعزيز علاقات التواصل بين اتحادات الطلبة في الموقعين.

مع بداية شهر أيار علمنا من اليوث ان آكشن بأننا حصلنا على تمويل للمشروع حيث بدأنا العمل على التحضير واختيار الطلاب المشاركين في الطرفين، بدأ الطلاب من فلسطين العمل على التقاط صورهم في بداية شهر تموز فيما شهر تموز فيما قتل الطالب معتصم (شاهدوا الصفحة الماضية) في بداية شهر آب .

التبادل والزيارة كانت في شهر تشرين ثاني حيث حل ثماني طلاب من جامعة القدس مع قائد للمجموعة ضيوف على لندن لمدة عشرة أيام قاموا خلالها بالتحدث وعرض ما أنتجوا من صور على طلاب جامعات لندن، في آخر يوم من التبادل تم تنظيم معرض للصور في جامعة سواس وورشة عمل تم خلالها نقاش قضايا التوأمات بين الجامعات والأهداف المرجوة منها وسبل تحقيقها للرقي بعلاقات التوأمة بين فلسطين وبريطانيا .

يجمع هذا الكتاب بعض الصور التي التقطت من قبل الطلاب الفلسطينيون والبريطانيون حيث يحوي متن الكتاب الصور الرئيسية التي التقطها الطلاب الفلسطينيون عن حياتهم تحت الاحتلال .

وقد خصص أيضا قسم خاص لعرض الصور التي التقطها الطلاب في بريطانيا خلال الزيارة.

فيما تتركز خاتمة الكتاب على النتائج التي خلصت لها النقاشات بين الطلاب عن الدور الهام الذي تلعبه التوأمات في تطوير الفهم والوعي والاحترام المتبادل للعمل المشترك في قضايا حقوق الإنسان .

The 'Look at our Lives' project

The 'Look at our Lives' project began in early 2011 when we worked with students from the Al Quds University and universities in Camden to find a way to strengthen student twinning. We decided on an exchange based around a photography project that would allow both groups to meet and focus on their lives and the similarities and difference between them. The project was to take photos to show the contrast between the lives of students in both places, to discuss what they found and to work to develop twinning links between university student unions.

In May 2011, we learned that we would have a grant from Youth in Action and began to plan in earnest and to select the students at both ends. The students in Palestine started working on their photos in July. The killing of Motassem (see previous page) happened in August.

The actual exchange took place in November, with eight Palestinian students and a leader joining students in London for ten days of exploration, photography and discussion. On the last day of the project, there was an exhibition of photos at the School of Oriental and African Studies and a twinning workshop, when we worked with students to think about the aims and practicalities of twinning links between Palestine and Britain.

This book pulls together some of the photos taken by the students in Palestine and in Britain. The main section shows pictures from Palestine taken by the Palestinian students and some short stories and comments. A contrasting section of photos taken in Britain during the exchange visit follows.

The final section of the book talks about about the power of student twinning to develop understanding, respect and collective work for human rights.

فلسطين

6

Palestine

8

Living in Palestine

18

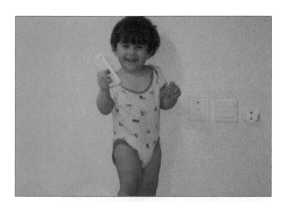

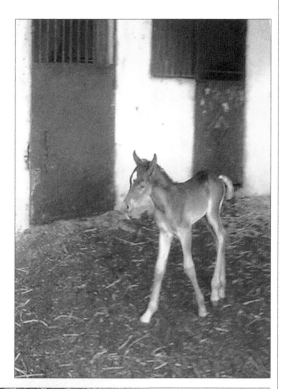

22

الدراسة في فلسطين
جامعة القدس

يكون بالعادة بين تموز وآب، وتتمتع الجامعة بمباني جميلة على تلال مطلة على مساحات مفتوحة من كل الاتجاهات، كما وتحتوي الجامعة على مراكز متخصصة في مجالات مختلفة ومتاحف للرياضيات والعلوم، لكن حقيقة وجود متحف لشؤون للأسرى تدلل على حجم الصراع داخل وحول الجامعة.

تناضل جامعة القدس من أجل الاستمرار تحت ضغط الحكم العسكري الاسرائيلي فجامعة القدس تحت اسم المدينة المحتلة والتي تحاول إسرائيل بشكل محموم السيطرة عليها وعزلها عن باقي مناطق الضفة الغربية، وعليه فقد عملت السلطات الاسرائيلية ولازالت على تغيير إسم الجامعة نفسها ورفضت الجهات الاسرائيلية الاعتراف بشهادات الجامعة حتى تقوم الجامعة بتغيير اسمها المرتبط بمدينة القدس.

عندما بدأت السلطات الاسرائيلية بالعمل على بناء جدار الفصل العنصري حول مدينة القدس المحتلة حاصر بناء الجدار جامعة القدس ودمر وجوده جمالية المكان، وكان على طلاب جامعة القدس التنقل لمسافات طويلة جدا حول الجدار للوصول الى جامعتهم في أبوديس، إذا تسنى لهم ذلك، وقد تم فصل مرافق الجامعة ومبانيها وكان على الجامعة أن تنقل بعض كلياتها من داخل مدينة القدس على اعتبار انه أضحى من الصعب جداً على طلاب الجامعة من حملت هوية الضفة الغربية من الوصول الى هذه الكليات داخل المدينة. وقد ناضلت الجامعة لمدة سنتين متواصلتين من أجل حماية الملعب الوحيد في المنطقة من تهديد ضمه وبناء الجدار عليه، كذلك فقد عملت الجامعة على تغيير المدخل الرئيسي للجامعة الى الشمال حيث كان المدخل الرئيسي يواجه الغرب قبل أن يبني الاسرائيليون الجدار أمامه مباشرة.

لقد جاء الطلاب الذين شاركوا في هذا المشروع من جامعة القدس، وهي الجامعة الفلسطينية الموجودة في مدينة القدس وتحمل اسمها، لقد بدأ المركز الرئيسي للجامعة بالعمل في سنة ١٩٨٤ في أبوديس وهي إحدى ضواحي القدس كذلك يوجد مبنى آخر للجامعة في بلدة بيت حنينا شرقي القدس، لكن كل الطلاب يتعلمون اليوم في بلدة أبوديس.

قصة الجامعة كقصة طلابها تحاول العمل بشكل اعتيادي لكن واقع وجودها تحت الحكم العسكري الاسرائيلي يتسبب في إعاقة عملها.

تحتوي الجامعة على العديد من البرامج والتخصصات الأكاديمية ببرامج بكالوريوس وماجستير، وتستخدم نظام الفصول الدراسية حيث تعمل من شهر أيلول الى شهر كانون ثاني كفصل أول ومن شباط الى حزيران كفصل ثاني بالإضافة الى الفصل الصيفي والذي

24

Studying in Palestine
The Al Quds University

The Palestinian students who took part in this project all study at the Al Quds University. This is the Palestinian university of Jerusalem and therefore named 'Al Quds' which means 'Jerusalem' in Arabic. The university's main campus was started in 1984 in Abu Dis, a suburb of Jerusalem, though there is another building in Beit Hanina in the East of Jerusalem. These students all study at the Abu Dis campus.

The story of the university is like the stories of the students themselves: it is attempting to go on with normal life but is disrupted at every turn by the pressures of existence under Israeli military occupation.

The University has a wide range of academic departments and issues bachelor's degrees and master's degrees, operates on the basis of semesters running September to January, February to June. There are summer courses each year between July and August. It has beautiful buildings on a hillside and an open-air auditorium. In addition to a number of special centres, it houses a maths museum and a science museum. But the fact that it also houses a Museum of Prisoner Affairs points to the struggles around and within it.

The Al Quds University struggles to survive under Israeli military occupation partly because its link to Jerusalem creates a challenge to the Israeli attempt to take over the whole of Jerusalem and to isolate it from West Bank. Israel has taken issue with the name of the university itself and refused to recognise the certificates of the students who study there unless they are issued in a name that does not connect to Jerusalem.

When the Israelis built the Separation Wall around Jerusalem, it built it across the campus of the Al Quds University in Abu Dis, and its existence dominates the place. Students from Jerusalem have to travel miles round the Wall to get to Abu Dis, if they are still able to manage this. The different campuses of the university are completely divided. The University had to move some faculties from Jerusalem to the Abu Dis campus as the West Bankers could no longer reach them. They had a major struggle for two years to prevent the Wall going right across the only sports ground, and they had to rebuild the main entrance to change its direction—it previously faced towards the Wall itself.

25

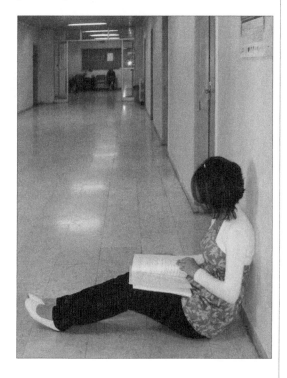

27

الدراسة تحت الحكم العسكري:

Studying under military occupation

Studying under military occupation

The context of the Palestinian students' lives is very different from that of British students. Some of the photos show the country they are proud of itself, with its Mediterranean geography, food and traditions and the ordinary life that people are trying to live.

But the things that the Palestinian students found most important to show the British students were not their personal life, their studies or even their leisure time. They chose their photos to show the the context of military occupation and the pressures it puts them under. They had no photographs of some of the things they described and offered comments and stories which also show the context of the human rights violations listed below and also the ongoing struggle against them.

- The **dispossession** of Palestinians and the **refugee issue** since 1948

- The **military system** that has controlled the lives of Palestinians since Israel occupied the West Bank and Gaza Strip in 1967

- **Huge areas of land being taken** from the Palestinians

- **Settlements**: new towns being built by Israel across the countryside of Palestine and currently extending rapidly

- **Destruction to the environment of Palestine** through settlement rubbish and sewage

- The **systematic separation and inequality** between the new Israeli settlers in Palestine and the Palestinian population – the difference in laws, treatment and access to resources that are often compared to apartheid

- **Confinement of Palestinians** to particular areas that are often compared to ghettos, through a system of passes and hundreds of military checkpoints all over the country

- The **Separation Wall** extending through Palestine

- **Violence** at the hands of soldiers, house invasion and arrest

- **Mass imprisonment** including 'administrative detention' (imprisonment without trial)

Further information

There is a lot of information on the internet all of these issues—you can start with:
- our own website **www.camdenabudis.net**,
- the UN office of the Co-ordination of Humanitarian Affairs in Occupied Palestinian Territory **http://www.ochaopt.org**
- the website of the Al Quds University to find out where these students study **http://www.alquds.edu/en/**
- the Right to Education campaign based at Birzeit University **http://right2edu.birzeit.edu**

For a simple book in relation to human rights in Palestine, please see our book **'For Hammam, A Handbook for Young People about Human Rights in Palestine.'**

الدراسة تحت الحكم العسكري:

إن واقع حياة الطلاب الفلسطينيون صعب جداً بالمقارنة مع حياة الطلبة من بريطانيا، بعض الصور المرفقة تبين جمالية البلد التي يعتز بها أصحابها بجغرافية متوسطية، عن التقاليد الفلسطينية والتراث والأكل والحياة العادية التي يحاول

لكن ما أراد الطلاب من فلسطين أن يوصلوه الى طلاب بريطانيا تعدى حياتهم الشخصية أو حتى دراستهم أو أوقات المتعة، حيث قدموا صور للواقع المرير الذي يعيشونه تحت الحكم العسكري الاسرائيلي والضغط الذي يسببه، لم تتوفر لديه الإمكانية لالتقاط صور لكل الأمور التي وصفوها والقصص التي رأوها والتي تعبر كلها عن مدى الانتهاك لحقوقهم الآدمية الذي يتعرضون له والضغط المستمر ضدهم.

- الترحيل الذي تعرض له الشعب الفلسطيني عام 1948
- نظام الحكم العسكري الذي يتحكم بحياة الشعب الفلسطيني منذ الاحتلال الاسرائيلي للضفة الغربية وقطاع غزة والقدس عام 1967.
- المساحات الشاسعة من الأراضي التي قامت إسرائيل بمصادرتها.
- بناء المستوطنات وهي مدن كبيرة بنتها إسرائيل على الأراضي الزراعية في الأرياف الفلسطينية والتي تتوسع الآن بشكل كبير.
- الأضرار البيئية الهائلة التي تتسبب بها مخلفات هذة المستوطنات من نفايات ومجاري.
- الفصل الممنهج بين الفلسطينيين والمستوطنين وبين الفلسطينيين أنفسهم، القوانين المختلفة والتفرقة في التعامل والوصول والحركة والتي تتصف بالتمييز العنصري.
- احتجاز الفلسطينيين في أمكان ضيقة أشبة بالجيتوهات والمعازل وتطبيق نظام للهويات في ظل انتشار عدد كبير جداً من الحواجز العسكرية في كافة أرجاء البلاد.
- بناء الجدار الفاصل والذي يتوسع داخل فلسطين.
- العنف الذي يتعرض له الناس على أيدي الجنود واقتحام المنازل واعتقال الناس.
- عمليات الاعتقال الواسعة والتي تشمل الاعتقال الإداري أي الاعتقال بدون محاكمة.

معلومات أكثر

موقعنا
,www.camdenabudis.net

موقع الأم المتحدة مكتب منسقيه الشؤون الإنسانية في الأراضي
الفلسطينية المحتلة http: / / www. ochaopt. org

موقع جامعة القدس
/http: / / www. alquds. edu/en

- حملة الحق في التعليم جامعة بير زيت
http: / / right2edu. birzeit. edu

بالإمكان كذلك متابعة كتب عن حقوق الإنسان في فلسطين الرجاء مطالعة كتابنا (الى همام كتيب للشباب حول حقوق الإنسان في فلسطين

الحكم العسكري

34

Military rule

الحواجز العسكرية

Checkpoints

الاضطهاد على الحواجز العسكرية

اشتكت طالبة من جامعة القدس على اعتداء تعرضت له من قبل الجنود الاسرائيليون، الفتاة تسكن في بلدة رأس خميس والتي تم عزلها بسلك شائك من قبل الاسرائيليون كجزء من جدار الفصل، حيث لا يوجد أي مجال للدخول الى البلدة إلا من خلال حاجز عسكري محروس من قبل جنود إسرائيليون، وقد أفادت الفتاة أن جندي إسرائيلي طلب منها رقم تلفونها الخاص وعندما رفضت ان تعطيه الرقم قام بمنعها من المرور من الحاجز الى بيتها لمدة طويلة ولم يسمح لها بالخروج من الحاجز إلا بعد أن أعطت الجندي رقم الهاتف وبعد أن تأكد من الرقم عندما أتصل عليه.

Harrassment at the checkpoint

A young woman studying law at Al Quds University complained about harrassment by soldiers. She lives in the village of Ras Khamees which is separated by a fortified fence, part of the Separation Wall. There is no way to get into the village except through a military checkpoint guarded by soldiers.

The student says that on her way home from university, a soldier wanted to take her personal phone number. She refused to give it to him, so he kept her ID and stopped her going through for a long time. He did not let her go until she gave him her number and then he rang to check it was her own. She had no other way to get home.

الجدار الفاصل

Separation Wall

اغنية الجدار

اللازمة :

لفيت وجهي شمال .. لقيت الجدرا
لفيت وجهي يمين .. لقيت الجدار
اتطلعت للشمال لقيت الجدار
اتطلعت للجنوب لقيت الجدار
مسلح ببطون .. مسلح بحديد
وليش يا رب .. عشان الذل يزيد

أرضينا حرقوها
عن الوجود زالوها
جبالنا غيروها
وديان سوها
حريتنا حطموها
بقفاص فرزوها
واحنا غضبانين
وبصدورنا كاتمين
كل هاد عشان
الي اسمو الجدار
جدار امانهم
وضمان ممتلكاتهم
الجدار مريحهم
من فلسطين مقاومهم
هيك هم ادعوا
وهيك ما بصير !

اللازمة :

لفيت وجهي شمال .. لقيت الجدرا
لفيت وجهي يمين .. لقيت الجدار
اتطلعت للشمال لقيت الجدار
اتطلعت للجنوب لقيت الجدار
مسلح ببطون .. مسلح بحديد

وليش يا رب .. عشان الذل يزيد
بعدين معك يا وضع
جد بدك ردع
احنا كثير كرفانين
ومن الجدار هربانين
كل ما قربنا منوا
بنلاقي صهيوني بدو
هويتناااااا!
هيهيه
واي هوية

هوية فلسطينية
ما الها اعتبار
وما الها اهمية
وكل الي صار لعيون
الحكومة الامريكية !

لفيت وجهي شمال .. لقيت الجدرا
لفيت وجهي يمين .. لقيت الجدار
اتطلعت للشمال لقيت الجدار
اتطلعت للجنوب لقيت الجدار
مسلح ببطون .. مسلح بحديد
وليش يا رب .. عشان الذل يزيد

48

Song of the Wall

Chorus:
I turned to the left.. I found the Wall
I turned to the right.. I found the Wall
I looked to the North.. I found the Wall
I looked to the South... I found the Wall
Armoured with cement... armoured with iron
And why, Lord? To increase the humiliation

They burned our land,
Removed it from existence.
They changed our mountains,
They flattened our valleys.
They destroyed our freedom,
They put it into cages.
And we are angry,
But holding it in.
And all because of this thing called the Wall.

49

The Wall for their security,
Protecting their possessions.
The Wall is keeping them at ease,
Shielding them from Palestine.
That's what they claimed,
But it's not right!

[Chorus]

We've had enough of this situation,
It needs to be stopped.
We're really fed up,
We need to escape from the Wall.
Every time we get near it
We find a Zionist who wants
Our identity
Haaaa
And what an identity.
The Palestinian identity
Is given no respect
And no importance.
And everything that happens
Is because of the American government.

[Chorus]

Anan Odeh

الفصل عن عائلتي

تحاصر بيت عائلتي في قرية النعمان بالمستوطنات وبجدار الفصل، حيث يتوجب على المواطنين المقيمين في القرية التنقل عبر حاجز عسكري للدخول الى بيوتهم، وهم لا يتمكنون من الدخول في كل الأوقات، التالي من أمي :

أنا أم عنان وأنا من قرية النعمان في القدس إننا نعاني منذ سبع سنوات عندما أود الذهاب لزيارة والدتي المسنة وهي التي ربتني ومنحتني حياتها وهي الآن مريضة وتعاني ولا يوجد عندها من يرعاها ويهتم بها أو يعطيها دوائها أو يطبخ لها. لا يستطيع أحد أن يكون بجانبها بسبب جدار الفصل، كنا ندخل البلدة من عدة اتجاهات لكن الآن كل البلدة معزولة بشكل كامل بسبب الجدار. لا يوجد إلا مدخل واحد للبلدة لكن الجنود الاسرائيليون يرفضون دخولنا عبره.

أود أن أذهب لزيارة والدتي ورؤية أخوتي، أحبذ أن أزور الأماكن التي تربيت فيها وكنت ألعب في طفولتي فيها لكني لا استطيع وأنا مستاءة جداً بسبب ذلك ، هذا كل ما استطيع قوله حتى في

الأعياد والمناسبات الأخرى لا يسمحون لي بزيارة أمي ، وقد أثر ذلك على علاقتي بأولادي.
عندما أذهب الى الحاجز وأنتظر لساعات ليشهر الجنود الإسرائيليين سلاحهم في وجهي ويأمروني بالعودة، لأنه ممنوع ولا يحق لكي الدخول، إنهم يفرحون لرؤيتنا نبكي بعد أن يرفضون السماح لنا بالتنقل.

أرجع الى البيت لأمضي وقتي في التواصل مع أمي عبر التلفون وهو أمر محبط لي وللجميع من حولي، وهذا يجعلني أفكر دائما بعدم الذهاب مرة أخرى لهذا الحاجز لأن هذا يعطيها الأمل بأني قادمة وتعيش على أمل حضوري تتأمل في أي لحظة.

الوضع الآن هو أننا لا نستطيع زيارتها وهي أيضا لا تستطيع القدوم إلينا وهذا ليس عدلاً، في جميع أرجاء الأرض هذا غير مقبول، نمط الحياة التي نعيشها نحن في بلد لا يحق فيه للولد زيارة أمة ولا للأم أن تزور ابنتها، أنا الآن ممنوعة من زيارة النعمان بلدتي منذ سنتين.

Cut off from my family

My family house in An No'man is surrounded by settlements. It's also surrounded by the Apartheid Wall. People who live there must pass through a checkpoint to get to their houses. But they are often not allowed. This is from my mother:

I'm Anan's mother and I'm from An No'man village in Jerusalem. We have been suffering for seven years when I want to visit my old mother that raised me and gave me her whole life. She is now very sick, there is nobody to help her or give her medicine or cook for her, stand by her and take care of her. No one can be beside her because of the Wall. We used to enter the village from different directions but now they are totally isolated by the Wall. There is way of going into the village and the Israelis prevent people from reaching the village.

I would love to go to visit my mother and to see my brothers. I would love to see the places that I used to go to and I was raised up in and where I used to play. That's all I can say – I'm very sad about it. Even on the feast days and on other occasions, I can't visit my mother. And that has an effect on my life and on my relation with my children.

When I go, I stand for hours in front of the checkpoint, the soldiers point their guns at my head and say 'Go back, it's forbidden, you are not allowed to cross.' They like to watch us crying after they refuse to allow us in.

Usually I go back home and try to communicate with my mother by telephone, which is depressing for me and for her. This makes me say all the time that I wish I hadn't gone to the checkpoint and waited there and given her the hope that I would be there soon.

The situation now is that we can't visit her and she can't visit us—this is injustice. All over the world, this is unacceptable, the way we are living. We are in a country and a place where a son can't see his mother and a mother can't see her daughter. Now I haven't been allowed to enter An No'man for two years.

أُجبروا على الرحيل

لا زال بإمكاننا الدخول عبر الحواجز.

وفي أحد الأيام تلقت جدتي قراراً مكتوب من الحكومة الاسرائيلية يبلغها بأنه يتوجب عليها مغادرة بيتها في غضون ٤٥ يوماً لأنها بعد بناء الجدار أصبحت تسكن خارج نطاق حدود بلدية القدس الاسرائيلية، وتهديد بأنها ان استمرت في السكن مكانها سوف تفقد هويتها المقدسية.

ولكي تستطيع جدتي الحفاظ على هويتها وعلى الخدمات التي تحصل عليها بعد دفع الضرائب كالتأمين الصحي قررت جدتي الرحيل من ضاحية البريد المكان الذي أقامت فيه كل حياتها، لقد كان هذا قرار صعب لقد تم دفعها الى مغادرة المكان الذي حمل ذكريات حياتها.

لقد كنت أعيش مع جدتي في منطقة اسمها ضاحية البريد والتي هي جزء من مدينة القدس، يحاول الاسرائيليون الاستيلاء على مدينة القدس وقد قامت السلطات الاسرائيلية بتقسيم الفلسطينيين من خلال إعطائهم ألوان مختلفة من الهويات، الأغلبية العظمى من المواطنين في القدس تم إعطائهم هويات ضفة غربية، وتم منعهم من قبل السلطات الاسرائيلية من دخول مدينة القدس.

لقد أعطى الاسرائيليون السكان في منطقة ضاحية البريد هويات زرقاء مقدسية، وهذا يعني ان لديهم الحق في الدخول الى القدس، لكن الحصول على هوية زرقاء لا يعني انه لا توجد مشاكل أخرى يواجهونها.

لقد بني الجدار وفصلنا عن مدينة القدس لكن على الرغم من ذلك

52

Forced to move

I used to live with my grandparents in an area called Dahyet al-Bareed which is part of the Jerusalem suburb. The Israelis are trying to take over Jerusalem and they divide the Palestinian people by giving them different coloured identity cards. The majority of people in the area were given green identity cards by the Israelis and are considered West Bankers, and the Israelis prevent them from going to Jerusalem.

The Israelis gave most people in Dahyet al-Bareed blue IDs. That means they can go to Jerusalem, but getting blue IDs doesn't mean we have no problem.

The Separation Wall was built and this divided us from Jerusalem, though we could travel there through the checkpoints.

One day my grandparents received a letter from the Israeli government that said, "You have to leave your home in 45 days. Now that the Wall is built, the place where you live is outside the borders of the Jerusalem Municipality. If you go on living there, you will lose your blue Jerusalem IDs."

So now, to keep their right to go to Jerusalem and their right to health insurance and the services they pay tax for, my grandparents have moved away from Dahyet al-Bareed where they had always lived. This was a difficult decision. They were forced to move and they moved all their memories with them.

Settlements

63

صعوبة التنقل

اسمي زكريا زعنون.... أنا طالب طب أسنان في جامعة القدس في فلسطين والتي تقع في القدس وأنا أسكن نابلس والتي هي بعيدة جداً عن القدس لكن البعد ليس المشكلة، مشكلتي هي أنه يتوجب علي السفر خلال أربع حواجز عسكرية اسرائيلية عدا عن الدوريات العسكرية التي في العادة توقف السيارات خلال توجهي الى جامعتي، لذلك فقد قررت أن أستأجر سكن في أبوديس بجانب جامعتي بعيد عن أهلي وأصدقائي، لم أكن أتوقع أن تكون فترة الدراسة بهذا الشكل كطالب فلسطيني، كنت أود أن أبقى مع عائلتي وأصدقائي في نابلس وأن تكون الحياة الجامعية من أفضل فترات حياتي .

لكننا لن نستسلم... سندرس... ونحاول أن نسعد أنفسنا.... ولن يستطيع أحد أن يسرق بسمتنا....

64

So hard to travel

I am Zakaria Zanoon ..... I am a dental student in Al Quds University in Palestine, which lies in Jerusalem, and I am come from Nablus city which is far away from my university. But it isn't the distance is the problem: the problem is that I have to pass through 4 checkpoints to reach my university and army vehicles which escorting us while we are in our way... so I preferred to find accommodation near my university and to be away from my family and friends.... This is not what I expect as a Palestinian student—I want to stay with my friends in Nablus—and my university life should be one of the most beautiful periods in my life!

But we will never surrender.... we will study.... we will be happy.... no one can take our smiles....

رحلة الى رام الله

لمسافة ٧٣٠ كيلو متر ويضعهم داخل سجن كبير، الهدف الرئيسي من بناء هذا الجدار هو عزل الفلسطينيين من سكان الضفة الغربية ومنعهم من الوصول الى مدينة القدس المحتلة، بعد ذلك فإنك تواجه حاجز قلنديا العسكري وستحتاج أكثر من ساعة كاملة من أجل أن تعبر الحاجز وعليك الانتظار .

في ذكرى نكبة فلسطين قررت أن أذهب الى مدينة رام الله للمشاركة في مظاهرة نظمت بهذه المناسبة، في المظاهرة رأيت نساء وأطفال ورجال من اللاجئين الذين ينتظروا العودة الى بيوتهم والتي تمت سرقتها في العام ١٩٤٨، واليوم وبعد كل هذة السنوات لازال لديهم أمل في العودة يوما ما .

في طريق عودتي التقطت مجموعة صور من المظاهرة حيث عانى الكثير من الطلاب من الغاز المسيل للدموع.

تقع مدينة رام الله بالقرب من مدينة القدس حيث لا تبعد كثيراً عن أبوديس، لكن عندما تود الذهاب الى رام الله يتوجب عليك السفر لمدة طويلة، لأنه ليس بوسعنا الدخول مباشرة للمدينة، الطريق الى رام الله تلتف مع جدار الفصل ومع المستوطنات ويقطعها حاجز عسكري والاكتظاظ الذي نواجهه على الحاجز.

في الطريق الى رام الله من بيتي ترى الجدار الذي يمتد في المناطق الفلسطينية ويقطع أوصال المواطنين الفلسطينيين

Journey to Ramallah

Ramallah is a city that is located next to Jerusalem so its not far from Abu Dis, but when you want to go there you will have a long journey because we can't go straight there, the roads wind round the Wall and round the settlements and are interrupted by checkpoints and the queues they make.

Going from my house to Ramallah you will see the Separation Wall. It is 730 km long, and it surrounds and cuts off all Palestinian areas and makes them a prison. The main purpose of this Wall is to stop the people from the West Bank from entering Jerusalem. You face Qalandya check point—you will need more than hour to enter so you will wait and wait.

On the memorial of Nakba day I decided to go to Ramallah to participate in a demonstration about the Nakba In that demonstration I saw women. kids.men who all are waiting to go back to their homes which were stolen from them in 1948, but they still hope to go back one day.

On my way back, I took photos of the smoke from the demonstration and many students suffering from teargas.

عن اللجوء

بحاول ينساها بسموم   راجعين يا وطنا .. راجعين نبني املنا .. راجعيين راجعيـــن
وكل الي مطلوب   راجعين يا فلسطين (الازمة)..ب
تكون لاجئ جامد
لاجئ صامد   سجل حياتي مشرد
للعلم راكض   كل يوم لمشاكل معرض
عشان بالمستقبل تكون قائد   بكل خطوة انا مهدد
من الدهيشة لجنين   جوا جدار عنصري محدد
وكل لاجئين فلسطين   فش طريق برة
بحق العودة بنطالب وكمان كمان بنحارب   حياتنا مرة
بفساد الامة والقادة الي مش مهتمه   بلا هوية حرية
بقضيـــانا .. نسيوا نسيوا اسرانا   كلو كلام ديموقراطية
جوات السجون الي حنو لصدر حنون ..   ضياع كامل
وكل هاد عشان صهيوني ملعون ..   عند جيل هامل
الي قلب شعبنا لظالم ومجنون !!   عندو كتير هموم

Song about refugees

We're coming back to our country...
we're going to have hope... We're
coming back, Palestine...

Record: My life is in exile
Every day I face problems
I'm in danger with every step
With the Separation Wall
There's no way out
Our life is bitter
Without identity and freedom,
Democracy is just talk.

Complete loss
For a neglected generation,
Which has lots of worries
But tries hard to forget them.
And all that's asked of you
Is to be a strong refugee,
A steadfast refugee,
To pursue knowledge,
So in the future you'll be a leader
From Daheisha to Jenin,
And of all Palestine's refugees.

Prisoner

I finished my towjehi in June 1999 and I started a degree in political science at Al Quds University. 7th November 1999 is a day in my life I will never forget. At two o'clock in the morning on that day, which was a very cold and rainy day, I heard a huge knock on our front door. At that time I used to have my own room on the roof of our family house. I woke up but did not know who that strange visitor was that came to knock at our door early in the morning like this and what big thing had happened to make someone come to us at that time of night.

At that time we used to be three brothers and four sisters and my father and mother in the house. It didn't take me long to find that our visitor was the Israeli army. Who else would come in this aggressive way to terrify people and to show off their power? 'The army which will never be defeated' against a family like ours, civilians living in peace. We did not have anything to defend ourselves except our determination, our dignity and our hope of freedom.

The soldiers managed to destroy the door even before my father could reach it to open it. An officer spoke to them and asked them to bring everybody in the house outside within three minutes. This time didn't allow anybody to get enough clothes to protect them against rain and the cold outside. Everybody went out except myself, because I was living on the roof of the house. Again the officer asked my father about me. My father told them that I was in my room, sleeping. They asked one of my sisters to come and call me and ask me to go outside.

When my sister reached me, she told me that everyone was outside and the soldiers wanted me to go out to the street.

I knew that they were after me so I wanted to use the time to put on warm clothes before I went out—this was my only chance as the soldiers had not entered the house yet. But just exactly as I put on my clothes, they started to call me from outside the house with loudspeakers, telling me to go out.

As soon as I went outside I saw laser spots all over my body: they were pointing their guns at me. At the same time they shouted on the loudspeaker that I should raise my hands above my head. As I went out, five soldiers jumped on me. They started to search me in a very wild way. They covered my head with a dirty cloth bag. I will never forget how bad it smelt. They tied my hands behind me with steel handcuffs. I still remember before they put the bag on my head that I saw five military cars and two civilian GMC cars (used by the special forces from the interrogation centre at Al Maskobiyeh). There were many soldiers surrounding our house and everywhere in our neighbourhood.

After that, they made me stand next to the wall of our house. I could hear different intelligence officers asking my family questions. I started to hear questions from two people at the same time, asking me a stream of questions but no direct questions I could understand. I couldn't understand what they wanted or what they were accusing me of. And two people speaking at once. They threatened that they would destroy our house stone by stone if I did not give them what they wanted, but they did not allow me to understand exactly what it was that they wanted.

After an hour of that interrogation, I heard my mother screaming from inside the house, shouting at the soldiers, asking what they were doing and why they were doing it to our house. So I knew that soldiers were searching the house and damaging things. After that, I managed to identify two people again coming to me and they introduced themselves as members of the Israeli intelligence. They said they were in charge of my interrogation, and introduced themselves as 'Uri' and 'Gali'. At the beginning, one of them said that I was accused of having a gun, and I had to give it to them or they wouldn't leave the house, and if I didn't give the weapon they would punish my family and keep damaging things inside the house. This went on for two and a half hours, while all my family members—except my mother, who had been taken inside—were still outside in the rain and freezing weather, and soldiers were inside the house going round everything.

After they finished searching and damaging things, a soldier took me to one of the cars which I identified from the sound of the motor as a GMC. Before I got into the car, the soldiers hit my head against the back door of the car and then pushed me inside, still wearing that bag on my head.

I ended on the floor in the car. There were many soldiers on the seats of the car. They started to kick me and hit me all over my body, and threaten that they would finish me in this car. I did my best to take my focus out of the car and start to think about different things because I did not want fear to enter into my head, I did not want them to destroy my mind.

The car started to move while I was lying on the floor of the car with the soldiers around me shouting and threatening, without any respect for the fact that they were dealing with a human being.

After that, we arrived at the interrogation centre which used to be a Russian church before the occupation, before Israel took it over and turned it into a jail and interrogation centre. There I was delivered to the people who would be in charge at the jail, the guards and the interrogation officers at the centre. The first thing I was asked to do was to take off all my clothes, even my underwear. I refused, so they started beating me all over, and they took my clothes off me. I stayed naked for half an hour while they were kicking me.

Then I was taken to the interrogation room, with my hands still tied behind my back and still with that bag on my head. Inside the room, they took the bag off my head and they made me sit on a chair which is less than 40 cm from the ground. They tied my hands and my legs to that chair. I spent ten continuous days almost without sleeping, except on that chair. Even the food that I used to receive I used to get on that chair, and the three meals I got took less than one hour in the day.

During the interrogation, they used to make pressure and to beat me. Then after these ten days I was sent to a cell for four hours in the night. After the four hours, I was taken back to the interrogation. For around sixty-one days, I saw nothing at all except the cell and the interrogation room. I was completely isolated from the outside world, and even when they used to move me from the cell to the interrogation room, they used to put that bag on my head.

After this period, I was moved to many jails, like Mejiddo in the north of Palestine and al-Nageb in the Negev Desert in the south of Palestine. And to Ofar in the middle, near Ramallah. And I was taken to court from time to time. I spent three and a half years without a sentence. In the end I was given my sentence, which was five and a half years and 6000 shekels fine and another full five years' conditional discharge.

I was released in September 2004 and I went straight back to my study, which I had not managed even to start before I had been imprisoned. But before I finished studying, I was arrested again, in December 2007. I used to work in a shop after my studies, and the soldiers invaded the shop, beat me and arrested me. I was sent to jail for five months.

Now I'm a masters student at Al Quds in international studies.

كان في الماضي قبل الاحتلال عبارة عن كنيسة روسية قبل أن تستولي عليه إسرائيل وتحوله الى مركز تحقيق وسجن، تم تسليمي الى الجهة المسئولة عن التحقيق من سجانين ومحققين في ذلك المركز وأول شي تم طلبه مني نزع جميع ملابسي حتى الداخلية فرفضت فردوا علي بالإهانة والضرب ونزعوا عني جميع ملابسي وكنت مجرد من جميع الملابس وتم تفتيشي بهذه الطريقة مدة نصف ساعة تقريبا.

أخذوني الى غرفة التحقيق مربوط اليدين معصب العينين ونزعوا عني عصبة العينين داخل الغرفة وتم ربطي بكرسي التحقيق بيدي ورجليه والكرسي لا يتعدى ٤٠ سم ارتفاعا مكثت في التحقيق على هذه الوضعية مدة عشر أيام متتالية تقريبا بدون نوم إلا على كرسي التحقيق او في فترة وجبة الغداء او العشاء او الإفطار وهي جميعها لا تتعدى ساعة تقريبا.

كانوا في التحقيق ينهالون علي بضرب وأيضا في الشتائم، وبعد عشر أيام وضعوني في الزنزانة مدة ٤ ساعات في الليل وبعدها أخذوني الى التحقيق ونفس الممارسات التي يمارسها أي همجي وعنصري كانوا يتعاملون بها مكث هكذا لمدة ٦١ يوما لم أرى فيها إلا زنزانتي التي لا تتسع لي والمحققين وغرفة التحقيق، كنت معزول بشكل كامل عن العالم الخارجي، حتى وقت التنقل بين الزنزانة وغرفة التحقيق كانوا

يوضعوا على عيناي عصبة او الكيس العفن كي لا أرى إلا الزنزانة وغرفة التحقيق والمحققين فقط.

بعد هذه الفترة نقلوني الى أكثر من سجن وهي سجن مجدو الساحلي الذي يقع في شمال فلسطين وسجن النقب الصحراوي الذي يقع في صحراء النقب في جنوب فلسطين وسجن عوفر الذي يقع على طرف رام الله الذي يقع في وسط فلسطين. في تلك الفترة أصبح سجاني ينقلني الى المحكمة تلو الأخرى ومكثت داخل السجن وأنا لم أحاكم مدة ثلاثة سنين ونصف وبعدها تم الحكم عليه بسجن الفعلي خمس سنوات ونصف وغرامه ماليه ٦ آلاف شيكل ووقف تنفيذ خمس سنوات لمدة خمس سنوات.

أفرج عني في شهر أيلول ٢٠٠٤ حيث عدت لدراستي في الجامعة والتي لم أتمكن من انجاز الكثير من الاعتقال كطالب في كلية العلوم السياسية ولكن قبل تخرجي وفي الفصل الأخير من الدراسة وتحديداً في يوم ١١-١٢-٢٠٠٧ وبينما كنت أعمل في محل تجاري بعد الدراسة قام جنود إسرائيليون باقتحام المحل والاعتداء علي بالضرب واعتقالي وقد حكم علي بالسجن لمدة خمس شهور قبل أن يفرج عني لأعود لاستكمال دراستي وانا اليوم طالب في الفصل الاخير من الماجستير في الدراسات الإقليمية في جامعة القدس.

سجين

أنا عبد الله عواد من بلدة أبوديس طالب في جامعة القدس أنهيت دراسة التوجيهي في حزيران ١٩٩٩ ودخلت كلية العلوم السياسية في جامعة القدس .

يوم ١٩٩٩/١١/٧ كان يوما لا ينسى من عمري لقسوته ففي تمام الساعة الثانية صباح كانت حالة الطقس باردة جدا وأمطار غزيرة، سمعت طرقا مفزعا على باب بيتنا كنت وقتها اسكن وحدي بغرفه على الطابق الأخير بين بيتنا، مرت لحظات ثقيلة وأنا أترقب ما يحصل ومن هو الزائر الغريب الذي يطرق الباب في ساعة متاخره جدا وما هي المصيبة التي حصلت كي يأتي احد الينا في تلك الساعة، في ذلك اليوم كنا في البيت ٣ أخوه وأربع أخوات وأبي وأمي .

بعد فتره قصير أيقنت ان من يطرق الباب هو الجيش الإسرائيلي الذي هو الوحيد الذي يفزع الناس ويتعامى ليعطي طابع الجيش الذي لا يقهر لأناس عزل لا يملكون سوى الإرادة والكرامة فقط والأمل بالحرية ونيل الاستقلال .

توجه أبي الى الباب قبل ان يتم كسره من قبل الجنود وتحدث له ضابط القوة الاسرائيلية وطلب منه ان يخرج جميع أفراد الأسرة من

البيت الى الشارع وأعطه مهلة قصيرة لا تتعدى ثلاثة دقائق حيث لم تكن كافية ليلبس ثياب مناسبة ويقي نفسه من المطر والبرد .

خرج الجميع من البيت ما عدا أنا لأني كنت اسكن في غرفه فوق السطح وعندما خرج جميع أهلي من البيت سأل ضابط القوة ورجال المخابرات عني فقال لهم أبي انه في غرفه العلوية نائم، فطلب من احد أخواتي ان تذهب وتناديني قبل دخولهم البيت

فأتت أختي وقالت لي أن الجنود يريدوك ونحن جميعنا نقف في الشارع في هذه اللحظة .

أيقنت انه يجب ان البس علي جيدا وأحصن نفسي للبرد قبل خروجي من البيت وهذه فرصه لم يدخلوا البيت، في تلك اللحظة بدأ الجنود بالصراخ علي بمكبرات الصوت من خارج البيت يطلبون مني الخروج من البيت بسرعة فخرجت لهم، وأنا افتح الباب توجت لجسمي أكثر من إشارة ليزر من بنادقهم وطلبوا مني أول ما شاهدوني ان ارفع يداي عاليا .

عندما خرجت امسك بي خمسة جنود وفتشوني بطريقه وحشيه وعصبوا عيناي بكيس نتن لا انسى راحته أبدا وربطوا يداي الى الخلف بكلبشات حديديه أنا أتذكر قبل تلبيسي الكيس العفن على راسي أني شاهدة أكثر من ٥ سيارات نقل جنود وأيضا حافلتين نوع جي م سي للقوات الخاصة التابعة لمركز تحقيق المسكوبية وعدد كبير من الجنود كانوا محاصرين بيتنا من كل الجهات والحي الذي اسكن فيه وكان هناك استجواب لعائلتي من قبل ضباط المخابرات .

توجه لي اثنين من جنود حرس الحدود وعرفوا على نفسهم أنهم ضباط مخابرات إسرائيليون وهم مكلفين بتحقيق معي وحسب ما اذكر أنهم أعطوني القابهم الأول قال ان اسمه)أوري(والثاني اسمه)غالي(قاما باتهامي بأني أملك سلاح ويجب علي ان أسلمه قبل خروج الجنود من البيت وإذا لم اسلم هذا السلاح سوف يتم معاقبة أهلي وسوف يتم تخريب البيت أكثر من هذا الخراب، وقد استمر التحقيق معي عند بيتي أكثر من ساعتين ونصف وهذه المدة جميعها كان أهلي خارج البيت تحت المطر والبرد والجيش يعبثون بجميع محتويات البيت، وبعد الانتهاء من التفتيش والتخريب أمروني الجنود بان ادخل الى سيارة عسكرية حسب ما سمعت صوتها هي جي م سي .

مع دخولي السيارة قام أحد الجنود بلطم راسي في باب الخارجي قبل ان يدفعني الى الداخل حيث كنت معصوب العينين، وجلست وكان من حولي جنود كثر يتراشقون عليه بعبارات سيئة وركلات من أرجلهم وأيديهم على معظم أنحاء جسدي بشكل وحشي وتهديد ووعيد أنهم سوف يقضوا عليه في النهاية، كنت بذلك الوقت افكر بشي بعيد عن هذه اللحظة كي أدرك أنهم لم يستطيعوا حتى الآن السيطرة على عقلي الباطني لأن ذلك كان هدفهم. تحركت الحافلة وأنا جالس على ارض الحافلة وحولي عدد من الجنود بتصرفاتهم الهمجية التي لا تحترم الحد الأدنى من آدمية الإنسان ولا كرامته . بعد فتره من ركوب الحافلة وصلت مركز التحقيق الذي

85

أخي الذي أصيب

بعد حوالي ساعة تمكنت من الوصول الى البيت بأمان حيث لا تبعد الجامعة عن بيتي بالعادة أكثر من خمس دقائق مشي .

أخي الأكبر سعد والذي هو أيضا طالب في الجامعة في كلية الاقتصاد كان في الجامعة ذلك اليوم ، وأتذكر أنني سألت والدتي عند وصولي الى البيت بأنه لم يصل بعد وقد بدا عليها القلق والتوتر ، حاولت الاتصال به على الهاتف النقال ولكنه لم يرد .

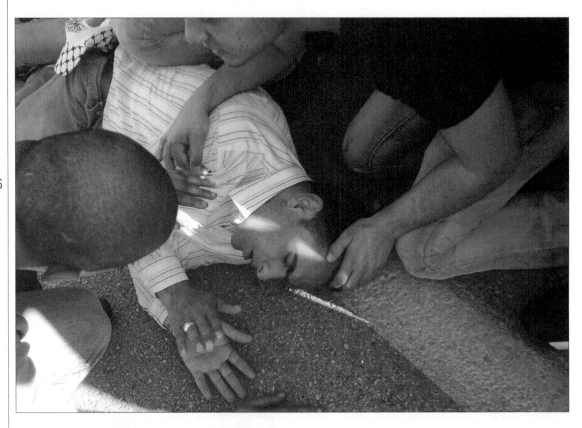

بعد فترة بسيطة جاء بعض جيراننا للسؤال عن سعد ما زاد من توتر أمي فقد استغربت سؤالهم عن سعد ، في هذه الأثناء وصلتني مكالمة هاتفية من صديق أخي أبلغني فيها بأن سعد قد أصيب برصاصتين مطاطيتين في الصدر .

لا أستطيع أن أصف شعوري لحظة سماعي للأخبار ، فقد كنت في غاية القلق على سلامة أخي ، لقد كان في طريق عودته من الجامعة الى البيت عندما قام جنود إسرائيليون بإطلاق النار عليه من دورية عسكرية مارة بدون أي سبب ، كان من الممكن أن يكون ميت الآن لكنه قال بعد ذلك أن الرصاصات أصابت كتبه قبل أن تصيب صدره .

لازلت أتذكر ذلك اليوم واستطيع أن أراه أمامي الآن ، لقد كان شتاء شهر شباط عندما كانت هناك مواجهات مع الجيش الإسرائيلي عندما قررت مجموعة من المتطرفين الصهاينة دخول المسجد الأقصى ، دخلت قوة عسكرية إسرائيلية بلدة أبوديس واندلعت مواجهات بينهم وبين المواطنين في البلدة ،، وقد قام المحاضرون في الجامعة بإلغاء الدوام لذلك اليوم وكان على الجميع التوجه الى بيوتهم ، أذكر كيف كان الطلاب يتراكضون من أجل التنقل الى أماكن سكنهم عبر وادي الجهير لتجنب الجنود الإسرائيليين ، بالنسبة لي أنا أسكن أبوديس وقد مشيت خلال الوادي الى بيتي ، وكنت أسمع أصوات الرصاص وقنابل الصوت في كل الاتجاهات وقد حاولت الاختباء عندما كان صوت إطلاق النار يقترب الى الوادي .

My brother who was injured

I remember that day as if I can see it right now.
It was winter time, in February. There were
problems in Al Quds because the Zionists
tried to enter the holy Al Aqsa Mosque. Israeli
military forces entered Abu Dis and problems
and demonstrations started. I was told by the
lecturer that he would cancel the lecture today
and students of the university tried to leave safely
through Wad al-Jheer valley. As I live in Abu Dis,
I walked through the valley until I reached home
and I could hear the noise and bombs clearly and
tried to hide when the sound become closer and
closer.

After maybe an hour I managed to reach home
safely although it normally takes five minutes to
walk from my home to the university.

My older bother Sa'ed who is studying economics
and financial studies was in the university on that
day too. I remember that when I reached home I
asked my mum about him and she was afraid and
answerd that he didn't come back yet. I tried to
call him but he didn't answer.

After a while, our neighbour came to our home
and they wanted to check if Sa'ed was with us.
My mum felt it was strange that they asked about
Sa'ed. While they were still in our home I got a call
from my brother's friend. He told me that Sa'ed
had been shot with two rubber bullets in his chest.

I can't describe how I felt when I got this news:
angry, afraid about my brother's health. He was
leaving his university to come home when an
Israeli military car passed and shot him for no
reason. He could be dead right now but he said
the bullets hit his books before hitting his chest.

Keeping going

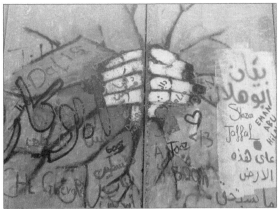

91

لندن

London

نظرة على لندن

94

Looking at London

98

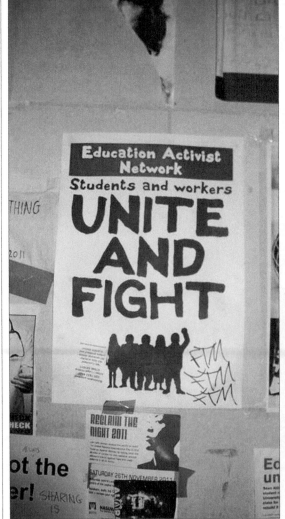

Studying in London

The impression of a Palestinian student

I walk among the green trees in London with complete freedom and without having to worry about military checkpoints that would destroy my time and energy on my way to university or on the way back. I scream: 'When will the Apartheid Wall be removed from around my university (Al-Quds University), and be replaced with a natural wall of trees? When will we in Palestine have universities of the same standard of those in London? When will every Palestinian be able to realise his dream of continuing his university studies?'

A student's time in university is a great opportunity to meet people, try new things and develop as a person. From what I saw, students in London are truly in the 'learning paradise' that we all dream of. I can't claim to know about all of the specialisations and the details of all of London's colleges, but I do really believe that the colleges in London are unique.

The college itself— meaning the people in it—is very friendly. Everyone is prepared to sit down and have a drink with you and help you. It is amazing having these universities and colleges in the heart of the city of London. It is amazing to see all the ways that the students are connected with worklife, restaurants, clubs. I can't stop myself imagining how it would be if we had a Palestinian university in the middle of Jerusalem.

Studying in London is very difficult. I noticed that an emphasis is placed on critical thinking and practical application. I also noticed the energetic participation of the teaching staff in designing the programmes that they teach, and the support they give to students.

There is a wide choice of subjects to study in the different colleges, giving students the opportunity to develop and to gain in-depth knowledge of these fields. There are also research centres of a very high standard, and many lecturers who are at the forefront of their fields of research. The universities use the most modern technology.

My love for libraries grew when I saw the various libraries in the London colleges, and how big and specialised they are – anthropology, medicine, dentistry etc. Every library has hundreds of computers and printers for students to use. The library also provides lots of extra services to the students, such as places for individual study, which provide them with the quiet and focused environment that they need. Students are also provided with electronic copies of books.

British colleges have lots of clubs and societies. There are meetings for every sport, religion and political opinion, as well as events such as mock trials, public speaking and debates. Most clubs are very cheap to join.

I am very happy. The trip to London was very useful, and I found many fields that I could pursue to continue my studies that are not available in Palestine, as we have a limited number of specialisations. We always had the opportunity to take part in interesting meetings with the English students and to present our own ideas about the topics we were discussing, so we made the best possible use of the time.

London is an incredible city, and a great place to live if you're a student. People often show you how important you are to them, and as a student you can get lots of discounts and special offers almost everywhere—at the theatres, cinemas, art exhibitions and even shops. It is impossible to be bored in London, and there are lots of opportunities to go out, night and day, any day of the week.

Visiting London taught me new skills— approaching problems, analysing situations, organising my time and working effectively.

Finally, I thank Camden Abu Dis Friendship Association for giving me this great opportunity to get to know a wonderful educational culture, which differs from the one I have grown up with in Palestine. I would particularly like to mention the people who organised the trip as well as the British students, who I want to thank for their hospitality and cooperation.

الكليات البريطانية لديها الكثير من النوادي والجمعيات.
وبالإضافة إلى ذلك، هناك مجتمعات لكل الرياضة والدين
ووجهات النظر السياسية، فضلا عن أشياء مثل محاكمات
صورية والتحدث أمام الجمهور أو مناقشة.
الأندية هي في معظمها رخيصة جدا للانضمام.

أنا في غاية السعادة كانت الزيارة الى لندن مفيدة للغاية،
ووجدت الكثير من المجالات في تطوير دراستي في عدة
مجالات غير موجودة في بلدي فلسطين حيث لدينا عدد
محدود من التخصصات، وفي لندن كان لدينا دائما فرصة
المشاركة في اللقاءات الممتعة مع الطلبة الانجليز، وتقديم
الأفكار الخاصة بنا إلى الموضوعات التي كنا نناقشها، وبالتالي
تحقيق أقصى استفادة من الوقت.

لندن هي مدينة مدهشة، ومكانا رائعا للعيش إذا كنت
طالبا الناس في كثير من الأحيان تظهر كم أنت غال عليهم،

وكونك طالبا يمكنك من الحصول على الكثير من الخصومات
والتمتع بالعروض الخاصة في كل مكان تقريبا. إذا كنت ترغب
في الذهاب الى المسرح، إلى السينما، إلى معرض فني، أو
حتى التسوق ارتياد النوادي، وخصم طالب دائما تقريبا تكون
متاحة.

من المستحيل بالتأكيد الشعور بالملل في لندن، وهناك الكثير
من الفرص للخروج، ليلا أو نهارا، أي يوم من أيام الأسبوع.
ان زيارة جامعات لندن أكسبتني مهارات جديدة – الاقتراب
من مشاكل منهجية وتحليل الوضع، وإدارة وقتي وجهود كفاءة.

وفي النهاية اشكر جمعية صداقة كامدن – أبوديس التي
أتاحت لي هذه الفرصة الرائعة لزيارة ثقافة تعليمية راقية
تختلف عما نشأت عليه في فلسطين وأخص بالذكر الأشخاص
الذين نظموا هذه الرحلة وكما اشكر طلاب الكليات البريطانية
لحسن استضافتهم وتعاونهم.

الدراسـة في لنـدن

ان من الرائع، كون الجامعات والكليات في قلب مدينة لندن كم هي مدهشة كل المشاهد المتشابكة التي تربط الطالب بالحياة العملية، والمطاعم والنوادي لا يمكنني إلا أن أتخيل وجود جامعة فلسطينية داخل مدينة القدس.

تتميز الدراسة في لندن بكونها جدية للغاية، والأهم من ذلك يتم التشديد على التفكير النقدي والتطبيق العملي من القضايا التي أثارت انتباهي. والمشاركة النشطة لهيئة التدريس في المشاريع الموجهة نحو السياسات المختلفة، وتقديم دعمها الكامل الفكري والبحثية للطلاب.

هناك مجموعة واسعة من خيارات الدراسة في مختلف الكليات والتي تعطي فرصة لتطوير واكتساب المعرفة المتعمقة في هذه المجالات كذلك بالنسبة لمراكز البحوث التي على درجات عالية من التميز وكثير من المحاضرين في طليعة من البحوث، وتشارك إدارة الجامعات في أحدث التقدم التكنولوجي.

انطباع طالبة فلسطينية

بينما وأنا أمشي وأسابق خيالي بين الأشجار الخضراء في لندن بحرية تامة دون القلق لوجود حاجز عسكري يقتل وقتي وجهدي عند الذهاب للجامعة و عند الإياب. وأصرخ متى يزال جدار الفصل العنصري من حول جامعتي –جامعة القدس ويستبدل بجدار طبيعي من الأشجار. متى سيكون لدينا في فلسطين جامعات على مستوى جامعات لندن؟ متى يستطيع كل فلسطيني تحقيق حلمه باستكمال دراسته الجامعية ؟

حيث وقت الطالب في الجامعة هو فرصة عظيمة للقاء الناس، ومحاولة تجربة أشياء جديدة، وتطوير الذات حسب ما رأيت

حبي للمكتبة ازداد توهجا عند رؤية المكتبات المختلفة في كليات لندن وكم هي كبيرة ومتخصصة – العلوم الإنسانية، والطب، طب الأسنان وما إلى ذلك كل الحرم الجامعي والمكتبة لديها المئات من الحواسيب والطابعات لاستخدام الطلاب. والمكتبة تقدم العديد من الخدمات الإضافية لطلاب الكلية، مثل أماكن دراسية خاصة الدراسة معزولة التي توفر للطالب جو الهدوء والتركيز الذي يحتاجه، كما توفر نسخا إلكترونية من الكتب.

فكونك طالبا في لندن هو حقا أنت في جنة التعليم التي نحلم بها جميعاً. لا أستطيع أن أدعي معرفة حول خصوصيات وعموميات كل كليات لندن ، ولكن أعتقد حقا أن الكليات في لندن فريدة.

الكلية نفسها – وأعني الناس – هي في الواقع ودية حقا. كل من هو على استعداد للجلوس وتناول مشروب معك ومساعدتك.

توأمة الطلاب مع
فلسطين

Student twinning with Palestine

What twinning can do

Strengthening student twinning

As a result of previous visits we have organised, university students' unions in Camden and Abu Dis have passed formal twinning motions in the past few years, but there has been little sustained contact between them. This project aimed to show how positive a link can be and to develop and extend student twinning between student unions across Britain and Palestine.

Reasons to twin—the right to education

For us in CADFA, this is part of our work that aims to promote human rights and extend understanding. Students in Palestine living under occupation face particular problems in achieving their right to education.

There are many different ways that people can be active on human rights. The particular contribution of twinning is the building of an on-going relationship, getting to know each other and the situation over time, the ability to focus on stories at the level of individual people. We think the interest in such visits as this one show its strength: people are interested in meeting their peers and thinking about how their lives might be like in another place. Active twinning links between people and organisations will enable many more people compare their lives and build positive projects to support those human rights.

Linking to your local twinning group

There are a number of practical problems with student twinning that have become evident in the past few years when the number of student union links to Palestine have grown across the country, partly through the efforts of organisations like Action Palestine and the Britain Palestine Twinning Network. One of them is finding and establishing contact with a potential 'twin'; another is to get the student union to vote in favour, a third is to maintain contact with the twin organisation, and a fourth is that the student population and the student union committees change each year and it is very easy for history to get lost and for links that had been active to become links in the past.

Twinning links between grassroots groups in Britain and Palestine have been spreading across the two countries in the past few years and they are linked together by the Britain Palestine Twinning Network. If it is possible for a student union to twin with the university in or close to the partner of their local twinning group, this can be an enormous support.

The two can really help each other. A Palestinian town and its university are very close and the two suffer from many of the same issues. A curfew will be on the university and the town. The Wall that cuts across a university also divides the town. The student prisoners from a university may live in the town. The checkpoints that people have to travel through affect everyone. So much of the effort of a 'town twinning group' and a student union twinning group can be in the same direction, making both of them stronger and more visible.

An active local group can help with contacts in the local area in Palestine. It can provide speakers, information, help when there is a visit and above all, a 'town twinning group' can help the student twinning to keep going for a period longer than the length of time that a particular group of students will be at university.

Our own example in Camden shows this: CADFA encouraged the twinning of SOAS and UCL students' unions with the Al Quds students' union, but our role did not finish there. We still provide active support in keeping both sides in touch with each other. This can be particularly important at the beginning of an academic year when old activists move on and new students have not heard of the twinning link. We can provide the history, photos, films and speakers from an on-going link, and the energy to organise projects such as 'Look at our Lives' which benefits the individuals involved and many other students as well.

Activities for your twinning link

Of course there are as many activities for a twinning link as your imagination. Just during this 'Look at Our Lives' visit there were discussions, speakers, a 'prisoner march' (small demonstration), a benefit focusing on Palestine, stalls, workshops and articles in student papers. It is important to have an activity every so often and it is important to have an exchange of news every so often.

You can draw on your twinning link for...
- Information about your partner for your university: speakers, exhibitions, films, facebook groups etc
- Communication to your partner—longest-lasting between groups rather than individuals
- Postcard-writing sessions, video conferences, blogs, formal communications between the unions
- Taking up particular issues
- Campaigning, demonstrating, lobbying when something happens to particular people in your partner university; using your detailed knowledge about the place to make a strong case
- Spreading the word widely
- Fundraising initiatives (benefits, sales, sponsored activities) that fit into student life and reach people who did not know about Palestine
- Visits to Palestine – organised by your union or by your local twinning group (or contact CADFA)
- Visits from Palestine working on projects not necessarily directly linked to Palestinian issues: for example, a women's visit can go beyond

the Palestine societies and link to women's societies, involving different people.

Keeping the focus on human rights

In addition to the practical questions laid out above there are further challenges to student twinning with Palestine from people who dislike the focus on Palestine for their own political reasons. They have used arguments that twinning with Palestine is political or unbalanced in order to frighten people from being involved and have tried to overturn student twinning decisions.

We suggest that the important thing to keep hold of is that this student twinning with Palestine aims to promote human rights. Human rights are meant for everybody. It is not necessary to link this work to political parties or to prescriptions about the outcome of the conflict in order to raise awareness of the importance of the human issues that are affecting students in Palestine and to extend British students' interest in action on this issue.

Resources

Your link to your partner will generate resources for you—photos, video, real stories.

There are some organisations you may get help from:
Organisations promoting twinning with Palestine
Action Palestine / Britain-Palestine Twinning Network/ CADFA
Palestinian human rights organisations including
Addameer / Al Haq / Right to Education Campaign

● مبادرات جمع التبرعات (المشاركة في معارض مبيعات وتبني نشاطات) التي تتلاءم مع الحياة الدراسية في فلسطين وتصل الى الذين لا يعرفون عن فلسطين.

● المشاركة في الرحلات الى فلسطين والتي قد تنظم من خلال مجالس الطلبة أو من خلال التوأمة المحلية في بلدك.

● الالتقاء مع الزوار من فلسطين والمشاركة في المشاريع التي ليس بالضرورة ترتبط بالقضية الفلسطينية بشكل مباشر، من مثل زيارات النساء الاجتماعية من فلسطين والتي ترتبط بالمؤسسات النسوية، ومشاركة فئات اجتماعية مختلفة.

إبقاء التركيز على مواضيع حقوق الإنسان:

بالإشارة الى الموضوع السابقة فان النشاطات التي تتقاطع مع فلسطين تجد بالعادة مقاومة من قبل الجهات التي تناهض الحق الفلسطيني لأسبابهم السياسية، لقد اعتادوا استخدام ذريعة العمل السياسي لمناهضة وصد أي جماعة تحاول العمل لأجل فلسطين ويطرحون كذلك قضايا التوازن في العلاقات مع الطرف الآخر لتخويف من يحاول التواصل مع فلسطين، وقد حاول هؤلاء كل جهدهم من أجل إلغاء اتفاقيات التوأمة مع فلسطين ووقف النقاشات حولها.

وهنا نحن نرى أنه من الضروري تحكيم القانون الدولي الإنساني وقوانين حقوق الإنسان في توجه الطلاب تجاه العلاقات مع فلسطين ويكون هدفها نصرة حقوق الإنسان. لأن حقوق الإنسان هي للجميع ولا ترتبط بأي نشاط أو حزب سياسي ولا تتقاطع مع مخرجات الصراع في سبيل رفع درجة الوعي والاهتمام بقضايا الطلاب في فلسطين ومن أجل زيادة اهتمام الطلبة البريطانيين للتحرك من أجل تلك القضايا.

مصادر:

علاقتكم مع التوأمة المحلية والتي ستمكنكم من الحصول على مواد من صور وأفلام وقصص حقيقية من الموقع. هناك العديد من المؤسسات التي من الممكن أن تساعدكم: مؤسسات تعنى بقضايا التوأمة مع فلسطين مثل آكشن فلسطين، شبكة التوأمة البريطانية الفلسطينية، جمعية صداقة كامدن أبوديس.

مؤسسات حقوق إنسان فلسطينية: الضمير، الحق، حملة الحق بالتعليم

المشروع "نظرة على حياتنا" والزيارة التي تضمنها كان هناك نقاشات ومتحدثين ومظاهرة للتضامن مع المعتقلين وكل هذة النشاطات تتركز على فلسطين، كذلك فقد عقدت الكثير من ورش العمل ونشرت كتابات من الطلبة الذين شاركوا في مجلات الطلبة، من المهم جدا ان يكون لدينا نشاط كل فترة ومن المهم كذلك ان يكون هناك تواصل وتبادل للأخبار مع الأصدقاء في الطرف الآخر كل فترة.

بإمكانكم طرح علاقات التواصل من خلال........

● معلومات عن شريككم توزع في الجامعة.

● متحدثين، معارض، أفلام، مجموعات على الفيس بوك.

● التواصل مع شركائكم من خلال مجاميع وليس فقد على صعيد الأفراد.

● كروت معايدة، كتابة مقالات، التواصل عبر الفيديو كونفرانس، عن طريق المدونات، التواصل الرسمي بين مجالس الطلبة.

● تبني قضايا محددة:

● حملات التضامن، التظاهر، حملات الضغط عندما يحدث انتهاك لحقوق أشخاص أو مجموعات في طرف شركائكم، اعلموا على استخدام معرفتهم عن المكان من أجل فرض قضية قوية.

● نشر المعلومات بشكل واسع للعالم.

ماذا تستطيع التوأمة أن تفعل

لقد انتشرت علاقات التوأمة بين الناس الشعبيين في بريطانيا وفلسطين على مدار السنوات الماضية من خلال عمل شبكة التوأمة الفلسطينية البريطانية، وهذا وفر الفرصة من أجل أن تدخل اتحادات الطلبة في التوأمة مع جامعات في الطرف الآخر بعلاقات قريبة من توأمة المدينة أو الموقع الجغرافي الذي تتواجد فيه وبأن تحتفظ بعلاقات مع ممثلي التوأمة في نفس الموقع حيث سيحصلون على دعم كبير من الموقع .

بعملهما معاً سيتمكن الطرفين من مساعدة بعضهما، فالجامعات الفلسطينية ترتبط بعلاقات متينة وقريبة من المجتمعات المحلية التي هي موجودة فيها لان المعاناة التي يواجهونها واحدة، فعندما يكون هناك منع تجول في الموقع الجغرافي فإن الجميع طلبة وسكان يعانون منه كذلك فإن الجدار الذي يعزل الجامعة يفصل البلدة، وعند اعتقال طالب فمن الممكن أن يكون قد اعتقل من مسكنه في البلدة نفسها، والأمر مشابه للحاجز العسكري الذي يعبر منه الطلبة والسكان للموقع نفسه، وعليه فإن معظم الجهد التضامني من التوأمة المحلية وتوأمة اتحاد الطلبة للجامعة سيكون في نفس الاتجاه وتنسيقه بين الطرفين سيكون حتما أقوى وأكثر فعالية .

إن وجود مجموعة توأمة محلية في الموقع الجغرافي يساعد في توفير عناوين للتواصل في فلسطين، كما يمكنهم توفير متحدثين ومعلومات والمساعدة عندما يكون هناك زوار من الطرف الآخر وقبل كل ذلك فإن مجموعة توأمة نشطة في الموقع تضمن الاستمرارية لتوأمة الجامعة لفترة أطول من اعتماد التوأمة في الجامعة فقد على مجموعة من الطلاب .

لقد أثبتت تجربتنا الخاصة في كادفا بأن التشجيع الذي وفرته لطلاب جامعة سواس وطلاب الكلية الجامعية في لندن في تواصلهم مع طلاب جامعة القدس حيث لم يتوقف دورنا في التشجيع . حيث لا زلنا نوفر النشاطات من أجل دعمهم للاستمرار والحرص على أن يكون الطرفين على تواصل دائم معاً، هذا طبعا ضروري جدا في بداية العام الدراسي في كل عام عندما ينتقل الطلاب الناشطين ويأتي طلاب جدد لا يعرفون الكثير عن التوأمة وعلاقات التواصل، وهنا نقوم نحن بتزويدهم بتاريخ العلاقات والصور والأفلام والمتحدثين من توأمة كامدن أبوديس في الموقع الجغرافي كذلك فمشروع مثل "نظرة على حياتنا" والذي يحقق الفائدة للأشخاص المشاركين فيه وللمجموعة العام في الجامعة نفسها .

نشاطات لتوأمتكم

بالطبع هناك العديد من النشاطات التي من الممكن أن تقوم بها توأمتكم والتواصل الفعال مع أصدقائكم، فقد من خلال هذا

تقوية توأمة الطلاب

كنتاج لزياراتنا التي نظمناها في الماضي، قامت اتحادات طلبة الجامعات في كامدن وفي أبوديس بتفعيل مناشدات كانوا قد تقدموا بها في الماضي من أجل الحصول على توأمات رسمية بينهم، حيث كانت هناك عوائق كثيرة من أهمها عدم وجود تواصل منتظم بين الطرفين، وقد جاء هذا المشروع من أجل إثبات مدى ايجابية هذة الروابط ومن أجل تطوير وتوسيع التوأمات القائمة بين اتحادات الطلبة في بريطانيا وفي فلسطين.

أسباب العمل في التوأمة- الحق في التعليم

بالنسبة لنا في جمعية صداقة كامدن أبوديس هذا جزء من العمل يهدف الى مساندة حقوق الإنسان وتعميق الفهم، حيث يعيش الطلاب الجامعيين الفلسطينيين تحت الاحتلال ويواجهون صعوبات كبيرة من أجل ضمان استمرارية دراستهم.

نحن نؤمن بأن هناك العديد من الطرق التي يمكن من خلالها العمل على قضايا حقوق الإنسان، وتبقى المساهمة الكبيرة من التوأمة من أجل بناء علاقات مستمرة، والتعرف أكثر على بعضهم وعلى الأوضاع المحيطة بهم على الدوام، حيث منحتهم هذه التجربة الفرصة للتركيز على القصص الشخصية للناس، نحن نعتقد أن الفكرة بحد ذاتها قوية ومميزة فالناس مهتمين كثيراً بأن يلتقوا ويتعرفوا على حياة أصدقائهم والتفكر في طبيعة الحياة لدى الطرف الآخر حيث أن التوأمات النشيطة بين الناس ستمكن الكثيرون من مقارنة حياتهم مع شركائهم وبناء مشاريع ايجابية وبنائه من أجل نصرة قضايا حقوق الإنسان.

التواصل مع التوأمة المحلية

تواجه توأمات طلاب الجامعات العديد من المشاكل التي تعيق عملها وقد أثبت التجارب الماضية بأن تطور علاقات التوأمة مع فلسطين وانتشارها ساهمة فيه مؤسسات مثل "اكشن فلسطين" وشبكة التوأمة البريطانية الفلسطينية، فإحدى المشاكل هي في إيجاد واستحداث روابط توأمة مع شريك مفترض، فيما يكون إقناع مجلس الطلبة بالتوقيع على التوأمة بشكل رسمي عائق آخر، ويكون الحفاظ على التواصل الفعال مع الطرف الآخر في التوأمة تحديداً بحد ذاته، أما رابع المشاكل فتكمن في أن الحياة الجامعية قصيرة حيث يتغير الطلاب في أي جامعة في فترة سنوات بسيطة وكذلك مجالس الطلبة تتغير في زمن محدود جداً كل سنه تقريباً وهنا يكون من السهل فقدان كل التاريخ وكل ما تم تحقيقه وتختفي روابط التوأمة وتصبح علاقات التوأمة من الماضي .

'Look at Our Lives' project reports

I think the project was a wonderful way of engaging British students with the harsh realities of student life in Palestine, whilst also providing space and opportunity to ask questions and learn more about the situation. All this was achieved in a happy and open environment. On a personal note I found a really firm friendship through this project, and am looking forward to visiting my friends when I return to Palestine in the new year.

I helped on various fronts during the Palestine-British exchange with Camden Abu Dis and SOAS Right to Education Society. As a member of SOAS Right to Education Society, I participated in various weekly meetings to brainstorm ideas for events and also distribute flyers about the exchange. Prior to the Palestinian students' arrival to London, I set up a Facebook Group Page called "Look at Our Lives -from Palestine to the UK" to help link both communities. I invited the students and the buddies to help facilitate the exchange in a more friendly atmosphere.

I learned a lot of personal stories from the Palestinian students. Some of the students told me about their hardships under the occupation. They explained to me the difficulties of getting to universities, visiting family and hanging out with friends. Also, a student recalled stories of interrogation and what he suffered during that experience. Lastly, I witnessed an exceptional moment with the students, when they watched the fireworks. Some of the students had never seen a firework display like that and others had seen them but it was conducted by Israeli state, when they celebrated their independence day. So, this time the students witnessed it without the emotional and political consequences that were directly tied to the fireworks.

What is great is that there are a few people from the Palestinian students that I am still in touch

with. Almost a month later, we communicate via Facebook and are still in touch. We are planning on figuring out a way for me to visit them soon! It was a great experience.

Participating in the 'Look at Our Lives' project allowed me to deepen my understanding of the daily hardships faced by Palestinian students in Jerusalem and to gain an appreciation of how lucky I am to have studied in England, with abundant resources and support, high quality teaching and easy access to facilities.

The project was skilfully planned and thought out, with clear objectives and a well structured timetable in order to meet them. I felt the day's goals and how we were to achieve them were always clearly presented.

The clear schedule for the visit also meant that buddies, hosts and other British students always had access to a timetable of activities. This provided a degree of flexibility for people wanting to join in just for an afternoon.

On a personal level, the most rewarding part of this experience was building personal relationships with all the students and my ' buddy' in particular. Hearing about the situation in Palestine from students at a similar stage in life to me really made the reality of their situation hit home. I feel I made friends with the whole group very quickly- they were all very open, friendly and fun to be around. Spending time with the students, sometimes talking about things nothing to do with Palestine, was an important and enjoyable part of the project for me. I would love to take part in a similar project again and it would be brilliant if we could organise a visit of British students to Abu Dis. I think that the most major improvement for the project would be in reaching a wider range of British students. Perhaps offering the chance of a visit to Palestine could be the way to do this!

During the ten days the Palestinian students were in London, they went to various universities where they presented different topics all related to their lives and how the Israeli occupation affects them. They related personal stories, which by personifying a difficult political subject were very effective, and they talked about these issues more generally. In addition to the 'official' talks, the students informally raised awareness by talking about these issues with their British based buddies, hosts and other students they met in London.

The Palestinian students took many pictures relating to a specific topic they had been assigned to, in order to compare these pictures of British student life with the pictures they and their peers had earlier taken in Palestine. These pictures were developed, and on the last Saturday presented in a photo exhibition at SOAS. During the exhibition, the students explained what the themes of the pictures were, why they had chosen them and what they saw as significant differences showcased by the pictures taken in London and in Palestine. It was an interesting and stimulating exhibition and many topics were addressed through the pictures, such as the difficulties presented by travelling to university via checkpoints, the Wall and the settlements.

I do think the exchange was beneficial to all involved. It gave the students the opportunity to share their experience with people who were oblivious to the situation, and for them to learn how many people did know about their struggle and supported them. For me, it had become all too easy to think of the Palestinians as a collective, so this was a chance to meet individuals and share what we had in common and hear individual stories. It was eye-opening and very special. I never would have been able to meet these students had this visit not been arranged, and I now have new friends that I will hopefully try to go visit in Palestine.

Exchanges like these are vital for understanding and the building of a world community. I was surprised how sad I was when I had to say goodbye to the people I had only known for a week, but I was genuinely sad to see them go and I miss them. This visit meant a lot to me, and I hope that future visits like this can be arranged for the future.

On our journey to Britain, we saw a lot of new things, the first time we'd ever seen them. The

visit for me was a unique experience: I learned a lot from it. It is important to keep going doing these students' exchanges. The main things that I liked on this visit were the opportunity to visit different universities and to learn more about the subjects that they specialise in. Also, visiting the museums there. Also the fact that we work to achieve twinning—it is very good for us as

students from Al Quds University and in general as organisations working in Palestine that we can explain to the whole world and specially in London and Oxford about Palestine and give information about our situation and the violations against our human rights. We managed to send a clear message and image about our life under occupation.

It is good that we managed to introduce our university Al Quds to the world and also to give information about the different faculties in it and the difficulties or the challenges which the university faces during its work. I wish that this kind of project can be repeated with other students from my university—it would be brilliant if there will be a chance to go to more countries to learn more about others' lives and to exchange information with them.

The most beautiful thing that I noticed on this visit was how kind and supportive and encouraging the British people and the British students are to the Palestinian issue, specially when I used to talk to people and everybody used to come to me and ask more and more questions and for more information about our personal case—Palestine.

اعتقد ان التبادل كان مفيد لكل شخص شارك فيه، لقد أعطى هذا المشروع فرصة جيدة للمشاركة بخبراتهم وتجاربهم مع أشخاص جدد يعيشون الواقع، كما كانت فرصة لهؤلاء بان يكتشفوا مدى معرفة الآخرين لواقعهم والصراع الذي يخوضونه ومن يساندهم في هذا الصراع. بالنسبة لي لقد أضحت الأمور أسهل لي للتعلم أكثر عن فلسطين بالمجمل، وأعتبر أن هذة الفرصة طيبة جداً لي للقاء أشخاص والتفاعل معهم وسماع قصصهم الشخصية. لقد فتحت هذة التجربة وسعت آفاقي تجاه العديد من القضايا، لن يتسنى لي أن أخوض هذة التجربة أو أن التقي بهؤلاء الطلبة لو لم يتم تنفيذ هذا المشروع. أنا الآن أحتفظ بأصدقاء عزيزين علي وأنا أتطلع الى زيارة فلسطين في أقرب فرصة.

فيها، كذلك زيارة المتحف كانت مميزة.

ان فكرة التوأمة التي نعمل عليها جيدة لطلاب جامعة القدس وبشكل عام لكل المؤسسات الفلسطينية حيث تمكننا من طرح قضايانا للعالم وخاصة في جامعات مثل جامعات لندن وأكسفورد وإعطاء حقائق ومعلومات عن حياتنا والانتهاكات التي تمارسها إسرائيل ضد حقوق الإنسان الفلسطيني، لقد استطعنا خلال الزيارة من إرسال صورة واضحة عن حياتنا تحت الاحتلال.

لقد قمنا بتقديم جامعة القدس للعالم وكذلك إعطاء معلومات

إن تبادل مثل هذا مهم جداً من أجل فهم وبناء علاقات مجتمعية عالمية، لقد كنت حزينا جداً عند فراق وتوديع الطلاب من فلسطين عند انتهاء الزيارة لمجموعة من الطلاب كنت قد تعرفت عليهم قبل أيام قليلة أو أسبوع، لقد كنت حزين لرؤيتهم يغادرون أنا افتقدهم جميعاً. لقد عنت لي هذة الزيارة الكثير وأتأمل أن تتكرر هذة الزيارات في المستقبل.

زيارتنا الى لندن

لقد شاهدنا في رحلتنا الى بريطانيا الكثير من الأشياء الجديدة لأول مرة في حياتنا، لقد كانت هذة الزيارة مميزة جداً لي وقد تعلمت منها الكثير وأعتقد أن تكرار واستمرارية نشاطات التبادل الطلابي مهمة جداً. من أهم الأمور التي استطعت تحقيقها هي زيارة مجموعة كبيرة من الكليات والجامعات في لندن وفي أكسفورد وقد تعلمت كثيرا عن المناهج والموضوعات المختلفة التي تدرس

عن مختلف المرافق والكليات في الجامعة والصعوبات والتحديات التي تواجه عمل الجامعة خلال عملها، أتمنى أن يتم تكرار مثل هذة المشاريع وأن تتاح الفرصة لطلبة جدد من جامعة القدس للتوجه الى لندن لزيارة الطلاب، كذلك فمن المهم أن يكون هناك تبادل مع بلدان أخرى للاطلاع على حياة الطلاب وتبادل الخبرات والمعلومات معهم.

أجمل ما في هذة الرحلة هو التشجيع والدعم الذي تلقيناه خلال هذة الزيارة والحفاوة والاستقبال من قبل الناس ومدى مساندة الطلاب البريطانيون للقضية الفلسطينية، لقد شعرت خلال لقاءاتي التي عدتها هناك مدى تفاعل الطلاب مع ما أقول من خلال الأسئلة الكثيرة التي كانت تطرح في المحاضرات المختلفة ومن خلال الأحاديث الجانبية التي كانت تدور ما بعد اللقاءات عن القضية الفلسطينية.

تقارير مشروع نظرة على حياتنا

لقد تعلمت كثيراً من القصص الشخصية التي سمعتها من الطلاب من فلسطين، بعضهم أطلعني على الصعوبات التي يواجهونها تحت الاحتلال، لقد شرحوا لنا عن الصعوبات التي تواجههم خلال توجههم اليومي للجامعات، أو زيارة أهلهم أو حتى التجول مع الأصدقاء. كذلك حدثنا طالب من المشاركين من فلسطين عن تجربته في التحقيق أثناء اعتقاله والمعاناة التي مر بها خلال تلك المرحلة، في الختام أود ان أقول أنني عايشت لحظات مميزة مع الطلاب فلسطين عندما رأيتهم يشاهدون الألعاب النارية حيث لم يتسنى للعديد منهم مشاهدة هذا العرض الهائل من الألعاب النارية فيما قال آخرون أنهم كانوا يشاهدونها خلال الاحتفالات الاسرائيلية بتأسيس دولتهم، وعليه فان الطلاب الفلسطينيون شاهدوا الألعاب النارية هذة المرة بدون الانطباعات السياسية والعاطفية السيئة والتي ارتبطت بالألعاب النارية في بلدهم.

أكثر ما هو مميز الآن بعد انتهاء هذا المشروع بشهر أنني لازلت على تواصل مع الطلاب من فلسطين عبر الفيس بوك ونحن نفكر الآن في أفضل الطرق من أجل أن نتمكن من زيارتهم في أقرب فرصة، لقد كانت فعلا تجربة مدهشة.

باعتقادي أن المشروع كان رائعاً في إتاحة المجال للطلاب من بريطانيا للاطلاع أكثر على الصعوبات الحقيقية لحياة الطلاب في فلسطين، كما وفر المشروع فرصة لنا من أجل إيجاد أجوبة لأسئلتنا عن الوضع هناك. كل ذلك تحقق في بيئة مبهجة ومفتوحة، على صعيدي الشخصي وجدت إطار جيداً لإقامة علاقة صداقة من خلال المشروع وأنا انتظر بشوق زيارتي الى فلسطين لزيارة أصدقائي في العام القادم.

لقد ساعدت كثيراً خلال الزيارة والتبادل بين فلسطين وبريطانيا مع جمعية كامدن أبوديس وحملة الحق في التعليم لجامعة سواس التي أنا عضوه فيها، لقد حضرت العديد من اللقاءات الأسبوعية ووزعت المنشورات الخاصة بهذا التبادل، وعملت على إنشاء مجموعة على الفيس بوك أسميتها (نظرة على حياتنا من فلسطين الى بريطانيا) من أجل المساعدة في التواصل بين الطرفين، كذلك قمت بدعوة الطلاب والأصدقاء من أجل المساعدة في خلق جو من الألفة والتواصل بين الطرفين.

مشاركتي في مشروع (نظرة على حياتنا) مكنني من تعميق فهمي عن الصعوبات اليومية التي يواجهها الطلاب الفلسطينيون

في القدس وفي أن أعرف كم أنا محظوظ كوني طالب في انجلترا مع كل الدعم والمساندة التي أحظى بها ومستوى مميز من التعليم وسهولة في الوصول الى المؤسسات التعليمية.

لقد كان المشروع منظم لأبعد الحدود وكانت أهدافه واضحة والبرنامج مبني بشكل مميز وان عملنا اليومي في التواصل مع الطلاب من فلسطين كان واضحاً، لقد شعرت ان الأهداف كانت متقنه وأننا عملنا على تحقيقها كل ما أتاحت لنا الظروف ذلك .

لقد كان البرنامج واضحاً جداً وشمل تحديد أدوار لأصدقاء وللدين استضافوا الطلاب في بيوتهم حيث استطاع الطلاب البريطانيون في كل المراحل من الوصول الى البرنامج والنشاطات في كل الأوقات، وقد وفر ذلك أريحية للجميع للمشاركة حتى في فعالية واحدة.

على صعيدي الشخصي أفضل جزء في هذة التجربة كانت بناء صداقات شخصية مع كل الطلاب الفلسطينيين وتحديداً تمارا صديقتي، كذلك الاستماع عن الواقع الفلسطيني من الطلاب الفلسطينيين والذين هم في نفس عمري والذي هزني بشكل كبير، أعتقد أنني أصبحت صديقة لهم جميعاً في زمن قياسي لقد كانوا جميعاً متفتحين ودودون، مجرد قضاء وقت مع الطلاب من فلسطين حتى وان لم نتحدث عن فلسطين كان مهم واستمعت به كجزء من المشروع.

أود ان أشارك في مشاريع مشابهة مرة أخرى وسيكون مميز جداً إذا استطعنا ان ننظم زيارة مشابهة من بريطانيا الى أبوديس. أتصور أن المساهمة الأكبر للمشروع هي إمكانية الوصول الأوسع للمجتمعات الطلابية البريطانية، ربما تنظيم زيارة الى فلسطين سيجعل العديد من الطلاب من بريطانيا يشاركون.

خلال العشرة أيام التي قضاها الطلاب الفلسطينيون في لندن زاروا العديد من الجامعات حيث قدموا العديد من المحاضرات عن حياتهم تحت الاحتلال الاسرائيلي وعن تأثير الاحتلال في كل مناحي الحياة، لقد شاركوا بقصصهم الشخصية والتي كان لها تأثير قوي في طرح قضاياهم السياسية، في نفس السياق فقد كانت المحاضرات الرسمية التي قدمها الطلاب مادة جيدة في تسليط الضوء على القضية الفلسطينية للطلاب البريطانيين من أصدقاء ومضيفين وكل ما قابلهم من طلاب لندن.

لقد قام الطلاب من فلسطين بالتقاط صور كثيرة عن مواضيع مختلفة من أجل مقارنة حياتهم بحياة الطلاب من بريطانيا من خلال هذة الصور والصور التي كانوا التقطوها قبل حضورهم من فلسطين، وقد تم اختيار الصور المناسبة حيث تم عرضها في معرض للصور عقد في جامعة سواس، وقد قام الطلاب خلال المعرض شرح المعرض للحضور عن مختلف الصور والمواضيع التي تناولها ولماذا تم اختيار هذة الصور وعن الأمور المختلفة والمتشابهة في الصور من بريطانيا وفلسطين. لقد كان معرضاً مميزا ومفيداً وقد فتح الباب لطرح العديد من القضايا والعناوين من خلال الصور من قبل الصعوبات بالتنقل الى الجامعات بسبب الحواجز العسكرية الاسرائيلية، والجدار الفاصل والمستوطنات الاسرائيلية.

CADFA

Camden Abu Dis Friendship Association

جمعية صداقة كامدن أبوديس

Camden Abu Dis Friendship Association is a human rights charity based in Britain dedicated to promoting human rights and respect for international humanitarian law in Palestine. Our work has focused on our link with Abu Dis, a Palestinian town in the East Jerusalem suburb that is currently divided from Jerusalem by the Separation Wall.

We have been developing a model of human rights education work, building creative projects that allow people in Britain and Palestine to meet and that give people in Britain a chance to hear the stories of life in Palestine. This has interested an increasing number of people in the human rights situation in Palestine. .

Our work falls into four main areas:
- Visits and volunteers
- Information: public meetings, publications and the website
- Encouraging friendship links and projects with Abu Dis
- Campaign work including urgent actions

In addition,
- we work to support and encourage other groups interested in twinning with Palestine to promote human rights, and we are active within the Britain-Palestine Twinning Network.

Our website is **www.camdenabudis.net**

تعمل جمعية صداقة كامدن أبوديس وهي جمعية خيرية موجودة في بريطانيا تعزيزاً لحقوق الإنسان واحتراما للقانون الدولي في فلسطين. لقد تم تركيز عملنا من خلال علاقات التواصل مع أبوديس، وهي بلدة تقع الى الشرق من مدينة القدس المحتلة حيث كانت تعد ضاحية من ضواحي المدينة وقد تم فصلها عن القدس بجدار الفصل.

لقد طورنا نموذج من التعليم في عمل حقوق الإنسان، من خلال تطوير مشاريع خلاقة تمكّن الناس من فلسطين وبريطانيا من اللقاء والعمل معاً، والتي مكنت المواطنين من بريطانيا من سماع قصص وتجارب حياة الناس في فلسطين، حيث انعكس ذلك على عدد كبير من المواطنين البريطانيين الذين تعلموا أكثر عن واقع حقوق الإنسان في فلسطين.

عملنا ينصب في أربع مناطق محددة:
- الزيارات والمتطوعين
- المعلومات: اجتماعات عامة، المنشورات والموقع الالكتروني.
- تشجيع علاقات الصداقة والمشاريع مع أبوديس.
- حملات التضامن والتحركات الطارئة عند حدوث انتهاكات.

كذلك
- فإننا نعمل على تشجيع مجموعات أخرى من أجل إقامة علاقات توأمة مع فلسطين وتعزيز الوعي حول قضايا حقوق الإنسان فيها، ونحن ناشطون في شبكة التوأمة البريطانية الفلسطينية.

www.camdenabudis.net

127

CADFA's other books:

128

STORIES FROM OUR MOTHERS
(Meetings of Palestinian and British Women)

English and Arabic. Personal stories telling of Palestinian women's lives and their experiences since 1947-8: stories of dispossession and refuge, loss and injury, love and courage. The book is testimony to the power of exchange visits through which British women discover the human rights situation of their counterparts in Palestine.

FOR HAMMAM—A Handbook for Young People about Human Rights in Palestine

Information in English and Arabic for young people about the human rights situation in Palestine. Structured as a practical handbook with reference pages on human rights, international humanitarian law and children's rights, the book begins with questions to stimulate enquiry and ends with a reference section and ideas of ways to be practically active in promoting human rights.

كتاب قصص من أمهاتنا (لقاء بين النساء من فلسطين وبريطانيا) هو كتاب باللغتين العربية والانجليزية يتضمن قصص شخصية لنساء عن حياتهن وتجاربهن منذ العام ١٩٤٧-٨ ، قصص الترحيل واللجوء الخسارة والجرح ، الحب والشجاعة . كذلك فأن هذا الكتاب شاهد على قوة التبادل في الزيارات حيث مكن النساء من بريطانيا من استكشاف واقع حقوق الإنسان في فلسطين لقد أعطى الطاقة والتشجيع للنساء للفئات الشعبية من أجل التحرك والعمل في التوأمة مع فلسطين .

"الى همام" (كتيب للشباب حول حقوق الإنسان في فلسطين) . يحتوي على معلومات عن واقع حقوق الإنسان في فلسطين ، وقد تم تصميمه ككتيب مع مراجع عن حقوق الإنسان من القانون الدولي الإنساني وقوانين حقوق الإنسان . الكتاب يتناول حقوق الأطفال التي اعتبرها الشباب مهمة بالنسبة لهم وقد تم استخدام كلمات وتجارب الشباب من فلسطين ، يبدأ الكتاب بأسئلة من أجل طرح القضايا وينتهي بقسم يحتوي مراجع وآليات عمل من أجل التحرك لنصرة حقوق الإنسان . الكتاب باللغتين العربية والانجليزية .

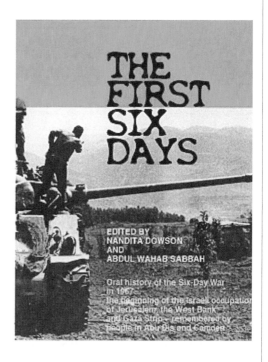

VOICES FROM ABU DIS—Living Under Israeli Occupation

Personal accounts by Palestinians in Abu Dis, now surrounded and cut off by the Israeli Separation Wall, military checkpoints and massively expanding Israeli settlements. These letters and stories sent to friends in Camden tell of the ways their lives are made miserable, desperate and impoverished by the Israeli military occupation, the military laws, theft of land, polluting of water, refusal of access to hospital, beating, imprisonment and killing.

"أصوات من أبوديس" قصص شخصية من أناس يعيشون حياة العزل جراء بناء جدار الفصل والحواجز العسكرية والتوسع الاستيطاني الاسرائيلي . هذة الرسائل والقصص ارسلت الى الناس في كامدن ليشاهدوا كيف هي الحياة للناس في أبوديس بعد ستون عام من الإعلان العالمي لحقوق الإنسان . لقد روا الناس عن الحياة القاصية التي يعيشونها جراء الاحتلال العسكري الاسرائيلي والقوانين العسكرية وسرقة الأراضي والمياه وعدم السماح للناس بالوصول الى المستشفيات والاعتقال والضرب

THE FIRST SIX DAYS—Oral History of the Six-Day War in 1967

In June 1967, the people of Abu Dis found themselves in the front line of the 1967 war, and this book of oral history contains people's memories of their responses as the war started and of their families' movements in its immediate aftermath. There are also explanations from Abu Dis of the context of 1967 and the effects of the war on the lives of ordinary people in Abu Dis.

١٩٦٧)الأيام الستة الأولى : ذاكرة أهل أبوديس عن حرب عام ١٩٦٧ – وبداية الاحتلال العسكري الاسرائيلي للضفة الغربية والقدس وقطاع غزة)

في حزيران مكن العام ١٩٦٧ وجد أهالي أبوديس أنفسهم في الخط الأمامي للمواجهة في الحرب، هذا الكتاب هو رواية شعبية يتضمن ذاكرة الناس عن الحرب وعن أسرهم وترحلهم المفاجئ من أجل حماية أنفسهم من نير الحرب . وقد تمت مقارنه هذة الذكريات مع ذكريات لأناس من كامدن عن نفس المرحلة، طيات الكتاب شرح لوجهت نظر الفلسطينيين في ابوديس عن رؤيتهم للحرب ١٩٦٧ .

نود أن نتقدم بالشكر الجزيل لمن ساهموا في إنجاح هذا المشروع...

الطلاب من فلسطين

عنان عودة

هيفاء الأنصاري

ابتهال أبو عامرية

سناء الخياط

تمارا هلسه

يونس السمان

زيد عياد

زكريا زعنون

الطلاب من بريطانيا

كاتلين بروكتر

أميلي دانبي

فيدال حرفوش

ميلاني بينت

نجلاء زيدان داوسن

سارة النويهي

صوفي سبان

ياسمين خلف

كذلك العديد من الأشخاص والمؤسسات وطلبة جامعات لندن الذين ساعدوا في كل مراحل المشروع

شكر خاص كذلك الى الاستاذ عبد الكريم بدر (الذي حضر الى لندن في زيارة تحضيرية للمشروع)

والى مايف مولوي (التي ساعدت في الصور مع طلاب فلسطين خلال فترة التحضير للمشروع)

وشوما بيجوم (إدارية ومساهمة متميزة خلال الزيارة)

وإيد فريدنبرج (مصمم الكتاب)

منسقي المشروع ننديتا داوسن وعبد الوهاب صباح

الكليات والجامعات واتحادات الطلبة والمجتمعات الفلسطينية في بريطانيا

جامعة القدس أبوديس

كلية بيسكس

كلية إمبيريال

كلية كينج لندن

جامعة ميدلسكس

جامعة اوكسفورد والمجتمع الفلسطيني وتوأمة أوكسفورد رام الله .

جامعة سواس

الكلية الجامعية اللندنية

جامعة شرق لندن

جامعة ويست منستر

كلية ويستمنستر كينجس واي

ونود أيضا أن نتوجه بالشكر الجزيل الى مؤسسة اليوث إن آكشن ممولي المشروع والى أعضاء جمعية صداقة كامدن أبوديس على الجهد الكبير الذي بذلوه خلال المشروع .

كما نتمنى كل التوفيق لتوأمات الطلبة الجديدة في جامعة القدس وسواس، والكلية الجامعية في لندن و(التوأمة الجديدة والتي جاءت كنتيجة للمشروع) جامعة ميدلسكس .

130

Thank you for your participation in the project to...

Palestinian students:
Anan Odeh
Haifa Alansari
Ibtihal Abuamriya
Sanaa Khayat
Tamara Halasi
Younes Alsamman
Zaid Ayyad
Zakariya Zanoon
British students:
Caitlin Procter
Emily Danby
Fidel Harfouche
Melanie Pinet
Najla Dowson-Zeidan
Sarah El Neweihi
Sophie Spaan
Yasmin Khalaf

And to very many others, particularly **students in London** who helped with the project in many ways.

Thank you for special help to
Abdelkareem Bader (who came on the planning visit),
Maeve Molloy (who worked with the Palestinian students on photography in the preparation phase),
Shuma Begum (admin and problem-solving),
and to the hard-working **members of CADFA**

Thank you **Youth in Action** for funding the project

Education and Culture DG

Colleges/universities/student unions/ Palestine societies involved
Al Quds University, Abu Dis
BSix College
Imperial College
King's College London
Middlesex University
Oxford University Palestine Society and Oxford Ramallah Friendship Association.
School of Oriental and African Studies
University College London
University of East London
University of Westminster
Westminster Kingsway College

And very best wishes to your on-going twinning links to the students at
Al Quds University
SOAS
University College London
and (new and a result of the project), Middlesex University

The project was co-ordinated by
Nandita Dowson and Abdul Wahab Sabbah
and the book was designed by
Ed Fredenburgh: ed.fredenburgh@mac.com

131

CPSIA information can be obtained at www.ICGtesting.com
Printed in the USA
LVOW011540020513

3470LVUK00003B/13/P